THE CROWN DISSECTED

THE
CROWN
Dissected

An Analysis of the
Netflix Series *The Crown*
Seasons 1, 2 and 3

HUGO VICKERS

ZULEIKA

First published 2019

by Zuleika Books & Publishing

Thomas House, 84 Eccleston Square
London, SW1V 1PX

British Library Cataloguing in Publication Data

A catalogue record for this book is
available from the British Library

ISBN: 978-1-999312-57-2

Designed by Euan Monaghan
Printed in England

ACKNOWLEDGMENTS

The author wishes to thank Tom Perrin for his customary wise editing, encouragement and support, and Bridget Harrison for commissioning another series of 'True' and 'False' articles about *The Crown* for *The Times.*

Also thanks to Laura Kincaid for copy-editing, and Euan Monaghan for designing the book.

INTRODUCTION

The Crown has now produced season 3, which covers the years 1964 to 1977. I appreciate that this is an immensely popular series, lavishly produced, well written and well acted. This means that it cannot be dismissed as tabloid rubbish. My complaint is that it is based on real and often living people, and while I believe that fiction can be a useful device to illuminate the truth, I am uncomfortable when it twists the facts and introduces themes that did not happen into the storylines.

Some will say that they can suspend judgement as to whether it is true or not and simply enjoy it as 'good drama'. I understand this point of view, and I daresay there are viewers who are intelligent and perceptive enough not to be swayed into believing that the fictional episodes are in any sense true. But I fear that many viewers do believe what they see. Indeed, since seasons 1 and 2 were aired, even some documentary makers are treating the storylines as true. One such asked me to discuss Prince Philip's distaste for kneeling before his wife at the Coronation, when in reality he was perfectly happy to do so.

Peter Morgan's statements to boost interest in the series

have also gone further than they should have done. Buckingham Palace recently issued a statement contradicting his assertion that courtiers had cooperated with him.

In writing this book, I seek to explain what really did happen, and thus show how some of the episodes are based on false premises. I used to think that the makers of *The Crown* were trying to get things right. As it turns out, they are happy to alter the facts in order to create conflict and drama.

I wonder if there is not a subplot here too. When Claire Foy was playing the Queen, it seemed that they were not building the Queen up into a person to be universally respected, while making the other characters emerge somewhat less than admirably. Viewers should be alert to the possibility of a Republican agenda.

It is not my place to review the portrayals in the latest series, though I cannot resist a few observations.

Claire Foy did a brilliant job in portraying the Queen, getting her subtle timing and delivery just right, and showing the many issues she had to face early in her reign. Olivia Colman's portrayal is somewhat less sympathetic. There is a restrained cheekiness in Olivia Colman which does not work for me in my understanding of the Queen's character. I found that she overdid the clipped accent, and I got bored with her many sullen faces and felt, perhaps unfairly, that she was trying too hard to get into what she perceived as the Queen's character, but not succeeding. Having watched all the episodes twice, I am left with the impression of a severe, cold and bossy Queen, which is not at all like the real monarch.

The new Prince Philip (Tobias Menzies) is rather a dull stick, though mercifully he has thrown off the overt cockiness of Matt Smith and he improves as the series progresses. Charles Dance, I thought, was magnificent as Lord Mountbatten – with much of the subtle menace of Ian Richardson in the 1990 version of *House of Cards* – and Erin Doherty has the alert feistiness and robust humour of the young Princess Anne. Josh O'Connor, as Prince Charles, portrays a spineless wimp, which is so often his fate in fictional representations. It is hard to remember that the real Prince Charles has parachuted into the sea, taken part in point-to-points and played polo with some vigour.

Marion Bailey failed to convince me as the Queen Mother – I got the impression that the film-makers did not much care for the Queen Mother, as they barely gave her a civil line. Helena Bonham Carter is a good actress. She plays Princess Margaret with considerable zest. She has given an interview to say that she was helped to understand her part by consulting the Princess herself, communicating with her from 'across the divide'.

Michael Thomas had a supporting role as the Queen's uncle, the Duke of Gloucester. The actor had a mane of hair unlike the late Duke and is addressed as 'Henry' instead of 'Harry', so it took me a while to work out who he was. The real-life Duke of Gloucester would not have been around much in the mid 1960s as he had a series of strokes and after 1968 was confined to his Northamptonshire home, Barnwell Manor, yet he keeps appearing. He died on 10 June 1974. Sadly, Michael Thomas himself died on 4 March 2019.

The Duke and Duchess of Windsor are given good actors. Derek Jacobi replaces Alex Jennings, and Geraldine Chaplin looks uncannily like the Duchess, albeit rather lined. (It is hard to believe that she is now 75 – it is half a century since *Doctor Zhivago*).

In season 2, the film-makers tended to take two events which more or less did happen and clash them against each other to make something that most certainly did not. This time they do less of that, but they hit on a theme they like and then cook up events to back up their thesis, regardless of whether they actually happened. An example of this is the conceit that Princess Margaret would have made a better Queen, explored and enforced with an exaggerated version of Princess Margaret's trip to America in 1965.

I lived through much of what is shown here, sometimes quite closely. I visited the Windsors' house in Paris the day before the Queen in 1972, and I was present at the Duke's funeral some days later. I knew quite a number of those portrayed here – for example, Robin Woods, Dean of Windsor from 1962 to 1970. I am also well documented, and so while watching the episodes, I have been freezing the frame and diving into a great number of books.

In writing these somewhat forensic notes on season 3, I have concentrated mainly on the made-up and misleading areas in the plot of each episode. There are also some areas where minor errors occur and since the budget is so large, I point a few out. I do appreciate how hard it is to get everything right, in respect of aspects of dress, orders and decorations – there was even a real-life Admiral at the recent State Opening of Parliament (14 October 2019) wearing simultaneously the riband and collar of the Order of the Bath (GCB), which is completely wrong. There are so many experts in different fields that it is hard to satisfy everyone. One viewer knows about aeroplanes; another is an expert on cars. When I was an extra in *Victoria & Abdul*, I was chatting to a 'royal footman' who told me: 'I'm a plumber in everyday life. When I see these plastic pipes, I know they didn't invent them until '55.'

A recurring annoyance in this season is the way Princess Andrew of Greece, Lord Mountbatten and the Duke of Windsor address the Queen as 'Your Majesty'. They are members of the Royal Family and can use her Christian name. Those that marry into the family like Lord Snowdon are not granted that privilege.

My final message is as before – fiction should help us to understand the truth, not pervert it.

Hugo Vickers

November 2019

SEASON 3

The ten episodes of Season III of *The Crown*
were released on Netflix on 17 November 2019.

EPISODE I

'Olding'

There are several themes in this episode. The first is the arrival of Harold Wilson as Prime Minister, elected in October 1964. The implication is that the Queen preferred 'Posh Alec' – the outgoing Prime Minister, Sir Alec Douglas-Home. The reality is that she will always work – and has always worked – with the elected Prime Minister of the day. Wilson features large in this series and is well played by Jason Watkins, but then Peter Morgan is sounder on politicians than on the Royal Family. Whether Wilson chose to lecture the Queen the way he does in these episodes is of course a matter of speculation.

There were all sorts of rumours about Wilson and his Russian connections, and this theme is explored – that he had been turned by the Russians and was known as 'Olding'. The suggestion that Wilson's predecessor, Hugh Gaitskell, was killed by being poisoned by the Russians – to clear the way for Wilson – is a new one to me. In this episode, the theory is sent up like a reared pheasant and duly shot down. As correctly stated here, he died of lupus.

They missed a trick since it is well known that Wilson arrived at the Palace, with his wife, children and his personal secretary, Marcia Williams (later Baroness Falkender). In this film, he arrives alone.

We are introduced to Olivia Colman as the Queen, as she examines a new head on the stamps submitted for her approval. This marks her development from young to middle-aged monarch. 'Old bat,' she says, which gives us an idea of how this fictional version of the Queen is presented. In our first sight of her, she is wearing the George IV diadem at her desk, which I doubt ever happens, but fair enough. We meet the new Michael Adeane, her Private Secretary, who struck me as looking the spitting image of Lord Casey, the Governor-General of Australia (who, as it happens, gets a mention in episode 4).

The next theme is the decline and death of Sir Winston Churchill, by then 90 years old. In this episode, the Queen is told that he has had another stroke; she visits him, alone in his room, and she listens to traditionally Churchillian pronouncements from him about Harold Wilson and his Russian connections at the time when he was at the Board of Trade. He tells her that Wilson was one of the first Western politicians to go behind the Iron Curtain. He drifts off to sleep. At this point the Queen tidies away his spectacles and kisses him: 'God Bless you, Winston.' A touching scene, but pure schmaltz. She would never have kissed him. Nor of course did she visit him after his stroke.

The truth is that by then Churchill was senile and incapable of coherent conversation. He had not had his stroke at the time of the General Election on 15 October 1964 – in fact he was just able to attend the Other Club on 10 December, though he scarcely knew where he was. It was a month later, on 10 January 1965, that he suffered a massive stroke, after which he neither spoke nor moved again. The Queen was kept informed of his state of health. He died at 8 a.m. on Sunday 24 January.

It is true that the Queen attended his state funeral (well done in this episode apart from the Queen being seated on the wrong side of the Cathedral, and a rolled-up belt masquerading as the Garter), but his death was not announced in the afternoon. We all heard about it on the radio, early on that Sunday morning, so there would have been no interrupting of a family birthday tea party.

Then there is Princess Margaret and Lord Snowdon and their failing marriage, which inevitably plays into the hands of the film-makers. I fear that Princess Margaret has been so traduced by tabloid biographers and TV documentaries that the real Princess has been lost from view. In this episode, there are scenes with an arrogant princess doing exactly as she pleases, staying in bed late into the morning, being humiliated by her husband at every turn, he not appearing at a lunch at the Mirabelle, stories of a maid having left due to exhaustion at her bad behaviour,

Tony supercilious or racing about London on a scooter, and Princess Margaret drunk at a party, tipping her cigarette ash into a glass of whisky. This portrayal is inevitable given the tabloid view of her, now fixed in the public mind.

A more interesting theme is the unmasking of Sir Anthony Blunt. This was more elegantly handled by Alan Bennett in *A Question of Attribution* in 1988, and there are echoes of that in these scenes – the arrogant art historian, disparaging about what he perceived as the lack of artistic appreciation of the Queen and of Prince Philip – and a lecture he gives, replete with double entendre. In these scenes, we find him exposed by the Royal Household, but kept on as Keeper of the Queen's Pictures for fear of a damaging effect on the British Secret Service, and relations with the Americans.

It also gives the film-makers a chance to further besmirch Prince Philip. There is a scene in which the Prince Philip character warns Blunt that he is a treacherous snake and he is on his case, at which point Blunt threatens to blackmail the Prince. Blunt points out that some drawings of him by Dr Stephen Ward had been found in his apartment following his suicide. If these were to appear, they would link a senior member of the Royal Family to the Profumo affair, the implication being obvious. I was rather hoping that the Prince Philip character would riposte that he could not give a damn. This was 1964 or so, and in truth a picture of Prince Philip, sketched at Buckingham Palace from life, had appeared as the frontispiece of *Illustrated*

London News on 24 June 1961. So that scene, which never happened in real life, was somewhat absurd.

Stephen Ward had quite a run with his sketches in the *Illustrated London News* in 1961. Other sitters included the Duke and Duchess of Gloucester, sketched at York House in June that year, as well as Princess Margaret, Lord Snowdon, the Duke of Kent, Katharine Worsley (later Duchess of Kent), her father, Sir William Worsley, Archbishop Makarios, Selwyn Lloyd, Roy Thomson, George Solti, Lord Adrian, A.L.P. Norrington (Vice-Chancellor of Oxford), Tunku Abdul Rahman Putra, Lord de L'Isle, VC, Keith Holyoake, John Diefenbaker and Henry Moore. Were they all involved in the Profumo affair? It is unfair to cast innuendo on the sitter on account of the morals of the artist. Augustus John painted the Queen Mother and Lucian Freud painted the Queen. They were good artists with less than exemplary private lives. Whether villain or scapegoat, Dr Stephen Ward was a good draftsman.

The Blunt episode suggests that Blunt lived at Buckingham Palace, which he never did – we see a disapproving Queen watching him coming back to the Palace (through the ceremonial front gates) late at night.

More interesting is the real-life question as to whether or not the Queen knew about his treachery. She did and there is conclusive evidence for this. When Blunt retired in 1972 he was not advanced from KCVO to GCVO as would normally have been expected. This was of some concern to his successor, Sir Oliver Millar, who went to see Sir Martin Charteris, the new Private Secretary, to ask if his job status had been demoted. Charteris told him not to give it another thought and on his retirement in 1988, Millar duly received his GCVO. Regrettably the Lord Chamberlain retained Blunt in what is called the Green Book (listing members of the Royal Household), before they could stop this, so in theory Blunt continued to enjoy certain Royal Household privileges.

As the credits roll, various captions tell us that Blunt was given immunity and remained in his post until 1972. One states categorically: 'The Queen never spoke of him again' – a brazen assertion. They do not tell us that he was publicly exposed in 1979 and stripped of his knighthood.

There are some minor errors. In a dinner-party scene, the Private Secretary would not have sat on the Queen's right with the Duke of Gloucester on her left. Nor would Tony Snowdon have kissed the old Duke at his supposed birthday party. (His birthday was 31 March, not 10 January, but there you go).

EPISODE 2

'Margaretology'

This episode begins with Tommy Lascelles informing Princess Elizabeth that she is to be prepared for her eventual fate as Queen after her father's death. In the episode, the young princess appears unhappy about this. They then create the fantasy that the young Princess Margaret wanted to be Queen in her place and that Princess Elizabeth supported this plan, believing her sister would do the job better. The storyline that follows explores this theme.

I am as sure as I can be of anything that Princess Elizabeth never wavered from accepting her duty. All she ever wanted to be was a pride to her father, and, as we know, she did not disappoint him. As for Princess Margaret, she was well aware that she was the younger sister, with all that that implies.

The episode focuses on the 1965 visit to the US undertaken by Princess Margaret and Lord Snowdon. So we see Princess Margaret setting off to the US, with Snowdon telling her that she is a natural number one, but that it is her tragedy to have been born number two.

Apparently one of the purposes of the visit was the promotion of a book of photographs by Snowdon (*Private View*, the proceeds of which, in real life, went to charity). They visit Lewis Douglas, former Ambassador to Britain (correctly depicted wearing an eye patch) at his ranch at Tucson, Arizona. Much is made of Princess Margaret as an outgoing personality, contrasted to a rather lonely and staid Queen back in London, bemoaning her lot to Prince Philip, and describing herself as 'dependable, predictable, reliable'.

We see a lot of the American tour, and at the end of it, the Princess Margaret figure returns home triumphant, apparently having secured a vital £1,000 million bailout from the Americans. She seeks to share the Queen's burden by taking on more duties, but the Prince Philip character tells the Queen that there are good dull monarchs such as her father, grandfather and Queen Victoria and by implication herself, and then there are the wild members of the Royal Family – Edward VII, the Duke of Clarence (referred to here as 'Prince Eddy'), the Duke of Windsor and Princess Margaret, and the episode ends with Princess Margaret both rejected and dejected. Then back to Lascelles ticking Margaret off and she running miserably to her room.

President Lyndon B. Johnson looms large in this episode, played rather powerfully and enjoyably as a complete vulgarian, with appalling language and bad habits – he issues instructions to his chief of staff, while poised noisily at the urinal. Apparently, he failed to attend Sir Winston Churchill's state funeral because Harold Wilson had failed to send troops to assist him in the Vietnam War. No. He had wanted to attend but was genuinely confined to bed with bronchitis, so the official US representation was Earl Warren, Chief Justice, and David Bruce, American Ambassador to the UK. Former President Dwight D. Eisenhower also attended as a wartime ally of Churchill's, who knew him well. Johnson did get annoyed with Wilson for not supporting him over Vietnam, referring to him as 'a little creep', but not until later.

In this episode, the Queen issues an invitation to Johnson to visit her at Balmoral for a weekend. The Queen says whatever is offered must exceed what she offered the Kennedys – which, in real life, was just a dinner because they happened to be in London. Curiously this invitation is issued on a formal card more usually employed for lunches, dinners or receptions.

There is no evidence that the Queen invited Johnson to Scotland. Furthermore, Johnson is told that no US President ever got invited to Balmoral. Funnily enough, Eisenhower was entertained there both in 1946 and in 1959. As it turned out, Johnson was the one US President between Truman and Trump that the Queen did not meet.

The Johnson figure is shown a picture of Princess Margaret and told to entertain her at the White House, and she is told to go. He does not seem to know who she is, though in real life, he had spent some time upstaging her at the independence celebrations in Jamaica in 1962, over which she had presided.

The film gives us a riotous romp through America, with Princess Margaret raving it up, getting drunk, having fun and bickering with Snowdon. The dinner at the White House involves a potential diplomatic incident in which Princess Margaret insults the memory of Kennedy, they have a drinking competition, they dance wildly, she plants a kiss slap on the President's lips and obscene limericks are exchanged (many of which have been relayed to and memorised by Wilson, back in London, and so he recites them to a sullen-looking Queen). Contemporary newspaper accounts reveal a rather more formal dinner at the White House, with staid speeches, on what was, as it happens, the President's 31st wedding anniversary.

So, let's have a look at what really happened. It is true that the trip was partly private and partly public. Much was revealed with the release of papers relating to 1973, when Princess Margaret's Private Secretary, Lt-Col Freddy Burnaby-Atkins, complained that a recent visit to Western Australia had lacked purpose. The then American Ambassador, Lord Cromer, en poste from 1971 to 1974, did not want her in the US because Sir Patrick Dean (he appears briefly in this episode) had warned him that her behaviour in 1965 had been controversial. The Private Secretary said she was keen to go to Canada or the US: 'She would, I think, take on anything challenging.'

In a memo Lees Mayall gave the Foreign Office committee on royal tours he explained: 'This is mainly due to the behaviour of some of HRH's friends, who tend to take such visits very lightly.'

Princess Margaret and Lord Snowdon had gone to America in 1965 after an invitation from Sharman Douglas, daughter of Lewis Douglas, which was the basis of Dean's reservations:

> They worked and played hard. It was a mistake that so much of their time was spent with and organised by Miss Sharman Douglas, though she did her best, after her own fashion, to make sure the visitors had a gay and amusing time. However, the keynote was the 'jet set' and it was not always possible to persuade the public that HRH and Lord Snowdon were serious as well as gay people. Hosts must understand that it does the royal party no good to turn the period of rest into a jamboree of actors and photographers, as was the case with the visit to the Douglas family.

In a debate on 4 February 1966, William Hamilton (the Labour MP for Fife West) attacked the visit, saying it had attracted 'public and private criticism' all over the Commonwealth. He cited high-society dinners and receptions, and quoted the *Sunday Express* describing it as 'a holiday frolic among the tinsel princes and princesses of Hollywood'. He queried the origins of the visit and its cost to the public purse. Twelve people travelled with her, and the whole of the first-class compartment of a BOAC plane had been reserved. He asked how many official duties had taken place. Christopher Warwick, Princess Margaret's biographer, gave the whole programme between 4 and 25 November seven pages in Appendix IV of his 1983 account of her life, which give a daunting list of engagements, and besides the glamorous ones that attracted media interest, there were visits to universities, 'the British Home organised by the Daughters of the British Empire', the auditorium of the Jet Propulsion Laboratory, etc.

Rebutting Hamilton's attacks, Walter Padley, the Labour Minister of State for Foreign Affairs, described the visit as an outstanding success: 'It began as a private visit ... Then it developed – and I emphasise this – as the result of Government and official interest, into a visit which consisted mainly of official and public engagements undertaken at the specific request of Her Majesty's Government.'

Small things – the President would have been at the steps of the White House. She would have called him 'Mr President'. Princess Margaret would not have been met by Wilson at London Airport and the Queen most certainly did not offer her the Order of Merit or the Royal Victorian Chain after this trip (Princess Margaret was pleased to be given the latter on her 60th birthday in 1990).

EPISODE 3

'Aberfan'

The Aberfan pit disaster was a particularly horrific event, Aberfan being near Merthyr Tydfil in Glamorgan, South Wales. It occurred at about 9.15 on the morning of Friday 21 October 1966, and 116 children and 28 adults died. It happened because a period of excessively heavy rainfall caused a build-up inside the tip, which caused it to slide downhill in a massive slurry – a black avalanche – engulfing the junior school and other nearby buildings. It was later proved that Tip 7, which covered the village, had been based on ground above water springs and that action should have been taken to avoid the disaster. The worst affected school was Pantglas Junior School where five teachers and 109 children were killed.

The full horror of this tragedy is played out on the screen. Those of us old enough to remember it can still recall the shock of that day.

In this episode, we see Harold Wilson arriving with

Marcia Williams (later Baroness Falkender) in an aircraft of the Queen's flight. We see Martin Charteris suggesting that the Queen might visit immediately. She and Sir Michael Adeane think not: 'The Royal Family visits hospitals, Martin, not the scenes of accidents,' says the Queen. She sends a message of sympathy.

Lord Snowdon goes to Aberfan. He did so in real life, explaining to Princess Margaret that he went because he was Welsh. (In this episode, he is more dismissive.) He reached Cardiff at 2 a.m. Like other visitors, he appreciated that he must not get in the way of the rescue operation, but he did sterling work in comforting the bereaved. In his diary account, Harold Wilson gave him 'the highest praise' for what he did. Later, Lord Snowdon told Anne de Courcy that it haunted him for years: 'It was probably the worst day of my life.'

This episode shows Prince Philip attending the funeral (on the Thursday) and later giving the Queen a moving account of what he saw. In real life, he arrived on Saturday 22 October, the morning after the accident. He did not attend the funeral.

The message relayed is that the Queen is sympathetic, but hide-bound by convention, and unwilling to budge. Here we see Wilson trying in person to persuade the Queen to go. She does give the real-life explanation as to why she did not go immediately – that she was reluctant to paralyse the rescue operation, for which there is logic. But a heartless streak is hinted at. When Wilson asks her to go and comfort people, she replies: 'Put on a show? The Crown doesn't do that.' She rings the bell to dismiss him.

On the Sunday, apparently the Queen, Queen Mother and Princess Margaret were all together at breakfast. (This was actually the day when the Queen opened St George's House, Windsor – of which more later.)

From here it gets worse. There are angry scenes in which the National Coal Board is blamed for the tragedy. Marcia Williams tells Wilson that all this was the fault of the Tories and that they need to capitalise on it, sidestep the blame, otherwise they risk returning to the thirteen years in opposition. She suggests spinning against the Queen. I found the Marcia–Wilson scene particularly unpleasant, and I hope it did not happen. I don't know how much spinning went on in those days, but we then see the Queen's three Private Secretaries informing her that the Labour government has sought to suggest that her absence indicates lack of care for the people of Wales and for the whole working class. Apparently, this forces her to go. She went with Prince Philip on Saturday 29 October, spending two and a half hours there, and was described in real life as being 'very upset'. In the series, Martin Charteris urges her to express emotion.

Back at the Palace, we see her tear strips off Wilson, who claims that members of his government may have broken ranks in briefing the media. The Queen tells him that she can't weep. There is something wrong with her; she is deficient. This provokes a lecture from Wilson in which he maintains that they should 'calm more crises than we create'. No one needs hysteria from a head of state. The Queen listens to the Welsh singing and the episode ends with a tear trickling down her face.

Mixed in with this sentimentality, there are some moving scenes – the rows of coffins, the funeral address, the flowers, the presentation of flowers 'from the remaining children of Aberfan'.

One nice touch in an otherwise grim episode – Wilson lights a cigar (he used to smoke a cigar in private – I saw him do so at a private lunch at the House of Commons in 1977 – the pipe was for the public – so a good touch by the film-makers, later expanded upon).

In a statement at the end, we are told that the Queen regretted not going to Aberfan more than anything else in her reign. Her various biographers have stressed this point. Ben Pimlott cited a former courtier saying she was not spontaneous, but 'regrets that now'; Sally Bedell Smith quoted her as saying: 'People will be looking after me. Perhaps they'll miss some poor child that might have been found under the wreckage', but somewhat condemned her, stating that 'her tardy reaction showed an unyielding side to her nature that would cause problems in the years to come'. Robert Hardman is more sympathetic, putting it down to 'a deep reluctance both to intrude upon private grief and also to show raw emotion in public'. Those who accompanied the real-life Queen to Aberfan remember that she was in tears.

EPISODE 4

'Bubbikins'

This episode has two clashing themes – the later life of
the Duke of Edinburgh's mother, Princess Alice – Princess
Andrew of Greece – and the challenges facing the Royal
Family regarding finance, and how they should relate to
the media – leading to the 1969 *Royal Family* film.

Having written the only authorised biography of Prince
Philip's mother – *Alice: Princess Andrew of Greece* (published in 2000) – I am well placed to sift truth from fiction.
The film-makers assign Princess Alice a character totally at
variance with her real nature, and they make her do things
which she would never have done in real life. As with a
previous television documentary, *The Queen's Mother-in-
law* (2012), she succeeds in rising above their mischief.

Looking first at Princess Alice, she did run a nursing
sisterhood in Athens, and she was always in quest of funds.
She based this on the convent in Moscow, created by
her aunt and godmother, Grand Duchess Elisabeth, but

the difference was that the Grand Duchess was rich and strong, and Princess Alice had no money and did not have the same strength and drive. She did her best, however. Here we see her selling a sapphire brooch – she did do that sort of thing. But needless to say, no police came to her convent, convinced that she was a fraud.

It is true that they were worried that there would be a coup in Greece and so she was brought over to London. This film makes a strong point that Prince Philip did not want her in the Palace, thought she was an embarrassment, feared that she would disrupt the *Royal Family* film, and when she arrived, did not even visit her. He tells the Queen that she has been in institutions most of her life (in fact only for two years). In reality, Prince Philip had been trying to persuade his mother to come over for some time. Only when his sister told her that the Queen had most particularly invited her did she agree to leave her apartment in Athens. She came over in King Constantine's plane when it next came to London for a refit. (Martin Charteris did not go and collect her.)

She lived at Buckingham Palace for two years between 1967 and her death in 1969, not in the rather dismal room this film assigns to her, but in a fine room overlooking the Mall and the Queen Victoria Memorial. I have seen this room.

The film-makers were right to have her bonding with Princess Anne. That was a lovely relationship. Princess Anne relished talking to her. She did smoke heavily, but I wonder if the point is adequately made that she was more or less stone deaf. (This only emerges later, while by and large she appears to hear most things.)

As for Princess Alice wandering out into the forecourt and getting caught up in the making of the *Royal Family* film, this did not happen. I don't think she moved around very much in those last years. And the scene in which she gives a long interview about her life is contrary to everything in her character. This is a device to trick the viewer.

The Prince Philip character finally deigns to visit her. We think he is going to berate her. Instead he tells her that she should have been greatly more celebrated, and that she is a credit to the Royal Family due to her saintly life. She discusses his 'dormant' faith with him. Interestingly, in real life, she did not press her religious ideas on him. At the end, off they go, arm in arm, for a walk in the Palace gardens. Another schmaltzy scene.

To give an overview of the relationship between Princess Alice and Prince Philip, he was the much-longed-for son, arriving in 1921, when four older sisters had been born between 1905 and 1914. Princess Alice adored him, but there were long periods when she did not see him, due to being hospitalised, then living remotely in Germany in the 1930s, and later in Athens. From time to time she reassumed the role of mother. I suspect that others in his family sought to minimise her influence on him. With the benefit of hindsight, we know that Princess Alice led a normal life for the rest of her days.

But her family could not have been certain that there would not be a recurrence of illness, and so they were always worried about her.

Prince Philip was with her in Athens just before the war, but steered into the British Royal Navy, in which he served throughout World War II. On his part, he was very good to her, often flying her from one place to another and, as related, buying her the apartment in Athens, and pressing her to come and live with them in London.

The film-makers have been selective in retelling Princess Alice's story. She was not 'treated' by Sigmund Freud, though he was consulted briefly. And nor, in a nasty flash-back, was she taken away by the men in white coats as a youthful Prince Philip clung tearfully to the car. She was taken away, but Prince Philip was kept away on a picnic with his grandmother. When they came back, she was gone. Frankly, that is bad enough.

So – to the *Royal Family* film. The episode opens with Prince Philip giving an interview in which he hints he might have to give up polo and that the Royal Family might have to move out of Buckingham Palace. This inter-view did take place – for NBC in America, but not until 9 November 1969 – some months after the film was released (in July 1969).

It gives the chance for Wilson to respond, saying that some of the Labour cabinet are hostile to the idea of an increase in the Civil List. He himself is conflicted. The film implies that the Royal Family are paid. They are not paid salaries, only expenses. The Civil List is for the running of their official lives, offices, etc.

In the film, Prince Philip summons Princess Anne, and she appears in her riding breeches. The actress playing her, Erin Doherty, has been given some good lines. He warns her of the danger of the Royal Family getting out of touch – the Greek Royal Family having been driven into exile – and tells her about the film they will make.

We see some scenes being filmed for *Royal Family*. And when it is released, according to what we are told here, it is a disaster, and given hostile reviews. The Queen is furious, Wilson thinks it was well received and there is a discussion about what image they should put across. Wilson thinks the Royal Family are not naturals on television. 'They don't want you to be normal,' he says. The public wants them to be 'ideal – an ideal'.

In real life, the film was well received, as noted by the Queen's various biographers. 'The film received ecstatic notices,' wrote Ben Pimlott. Sally Bedell Smith pointed out that 400 million people saw it in 130 different countries and 'the reaction of the public was overwhelmingly positive'. Robert Hardman quoted Sir William Heseltine, one of the private secretaries and a key instigator of it, as saying: 'It was a fantastic success … You couldn't go into the seventies ignoring television as they'd done in the fifties and sixties.'

It is strange therefore that this episode says the opposite, and leads into a scenario in which Princess Anne dodges her interview and pops her grandmother into the room instead. According to this episode, the Queen prevents international distribution and a BBC repeat. Yet after the BBC showed it, ITV then did so and it is anticipated that 68 per cent of the British public saw it.

It is true that now it is not allowed to be seen. I myself saw it several times, back in 1969.

Small points – the Tsar of Russia was Princess Alice's uncle, not great-uncle. As stated, Princess Alice would not call her daughter-in-law 'Your Majesty'. She did call Prince Philip 'Bubbikins' when he was young.

Prince Philip wears the GBE neck badge, though after 1968 he had the Order of Merit. To be fair, he wears the OM in later episodes. Other details of decorations are correct.

EPISODE 5

'Coup'

The coup episode is based on a strange incident in 1968, three years after Mountbatten retired as Chief of the Defence Staff.

According to his authorised biographer, Philip Ziegler, Hugh Cudlipp, Editorial Director of the *Daily Mirror,* visited Mountbatten at Broadlands in May 1968 and they discussed 'the dangerous decline in national morale'. Cudlipp then fixed a meeting with his boss at the *Daily Mirror,* Cecil King, at Mountbatten's London flat in Kinnerton Street, and Mountbatten invited his friend, Sir Solly Zuckerman, along to make sure that nothing got out of control. There is more than one version of what happened. Mountbatten, Cudlipp and Zuckerman agreed that King inveighed against Wilson's government and suggested that the situation could decline into anarchy with bloodshed in the streets, and tried to persuade Mountbatten to be prepared to take over and lead a Government of

National Unity should that happen. Zuckerman said it was rank treachery and stormed out. Mountbatten said he could not contemplate such an outrageous proposition.

Cecil King's version was different. He maintained that Mountbatten said the Queen was worried about the state of the nation and that he did not seem averse to stepping forward. Mountbatten's reputation was somewhat smeared by implication. Since nothing came of the proposed coup, who did what does not matter much.

This episode gives us a version of this. Mountbatten is to be kicked out as Chief of the Defence Staff, to get Wilson good headlines. They describe him as 'crooked, vain and power mad'. As relayed, Mountbatten retired in 1965. Cecil King cooks up an idea to make use of him, making the point that when one door closes, another opens.

Mountbatten is convinced that the modern government is no good. We see him giving a talk about past glories and leading his audience of veterans into reciting "The Road to Mandalay". Cecil King is there. He wants to see him. And he invites him to lunch at Threadneedle Street. Cecil King prompts Mountbatten that Wilson needs to be overthrown, and that he, Mountbatten, should be the respected figure to be an interim leader and head an emergency government. His first reaction is to say he could not contemplate such a thing. But he wavers: 'This is all very interesting.' He asks for 48 hours.

Concurrent to this is an examination of the Queen and her racing. Her horse, Apprentice, fails to win at Royal

Ascot, and Lord Porchester advises her to branch out more globally in order to compete better with the Aga Khan. The Queen heads off for about two weeks (in real life just a day or two), first to Normandy and later to Kentucky, which extends into an entire month away. The real Queen has never neglected her duties as monarch by going abroad for a month for purely private reasons.

The Queen has only ever travelled abroad privately in connection with equestrian interests, but only for a few days in total, not weeks on end as in this film. But it gives the film-makers the chance to emphasise that if she were not Queen, then she would prefer to be a country woman, breeding racehorses. When she hears that Mountbatten might be plotting against her elected Prime Minister she immediately returns home from this month-long joyride.

In this series, there are rather a lot of scenes in which a fierce Queen summons some retrograde figure and tears strips off him. This time it is Mountbatten. She tells him that, instead of organising coups, he is better employed acting as a father figure to Philip, an uncle to her, a king-maker to Charles and a brother to his own sister, Alice. He duly visits Princess Alice and she tells him they are figures from another age with no relevance to today.

There is then a reconciliation scene with Prince Philip, welcoming the Queen back from her month away. Small points – Mountbatten's uniform is pretty good. Maybe the GCB riband is too purple and the Garter collar is hopeless – they dressed him as the real-life Mountbatten was dressed for the Silver Jubilee in 1977. His real-life retirement scene found him with Garter riband as in the portrait carried out after him.

When the Sovereign leaves the country, six Counsellors of State are appointed and two of them act in tandem. Therefore, the Queen Mother would not be running the country on her own, as suggested here.

EPISODE 6

'Tywysog Cymru'

Episode 6 introduces Prince Charles taking part in theatricals at Cambridge. The episode covers his Investiture as Prince of Wales at Caernarvon Castle in July 1969. It involves him being moved from Cambridge for a stint at Aberystwyth University. All this did happen, and unlike other episodes it is closer to the truth, though it introduces one or two speculative themes.

The Earl Marshal, the Duke of Norfolk, and Sir Michael Adeane tell Wilson's cabinet that the Investiture will be a traditional ceremony with a considerable military presence. Wilson tells the po-faced Queen it would be less of an Investiture 'and more like an invasion'. In fact, the ceremony was modernised by Lord Snowdon, and there had only ever been one such before – in recent times – in 1911 for Edward, Prince of Wales, son of George V.

It is decided that Prince Charles will go to Aberystwyth for political reasons, so that he can identify himself as a 'true native son of Wales' and learn some words of Welsh. The Queen thinks he should stay at Cambridge. Wilson wants him there to dampen down hostile nationalist feelings. So he is confronted by a phalanx of the Royal Family, led by the Queen, who tells him where his duty lies. Played as a forlorn figure by Josh O'Connor, loose of chin and slightly jug-eared, he is miserable at the prospect and tearful. The Princess Anne figure gives him a kiss and then a punch in the stomach to stiffen his resolve. In truth, the Aberystwyth decision had been taken two years before by George Thomas, Secretary of State for Wales.

He arrives at Aberystwyth at a time when Welsh nationalism is prevalent – this is true – he did. He meets Sir Ben Bowen Thomas and is assigned a tutor, who is distinctly anti-Royal, called Mr (in fact Dr) Tedi Millward, Vice-President of Plaid Cymru (born in 1930 and still alive). This is also true. Years later Millward recalled:

The early '60s was the start of an upsurge in Welsh nationalism that saw the first Plaid Cymru politician elected to parliament – Gwynfor Evans, in 1966. By that point I was a well-known nationalist, so I was a little surprised when the university asked me if I would teach Welsh to Prince Charles, for a term, in 1969. This was ahead of his investiture as Prince of Wales in July. He had a one-on-one tutorial with me once a week. He was eager, and did a lot of talking. By the end, his accent was quite good. Toward the end of his term, he said good morning – 'bore da' – to a woman at college; she turned to him and said: 'I don't speak Welsh!' His presence caused a bit of a stir. Crowds would gather outside the college as he drove up in his sports car.

In this episode Millward does not want the job. 'You can't make me do this.' But he does, realising that the Prince will make his speech in Welsh.

Prince Charles arrives in a chauffeur-driven Rolls-Royce, greeted by protestors. (As noted, he drove his own sports car.) Millward welcomes him as 'Charles' and they have a discussion as to whether the Crown threatens Welsh identity by imposing Britishness. We see him in the language laboratory, to learn Welsh. We see him in a grim student room. Other students are reluctant to engage with him – a door is slammed in his face. We see him solitary with his cello as rock music blares from the next-door room. He pleads his misery to his sister who urges: 'chin up'.

He goes down badly at a college dinner – he reveals he has not yet been to the library. Llywelyn ap Gruffydd is mentioned – he shocks the table by not knowing who he is – a predecessor as Prince of Wales between 1258 and 1282.

Next day his tutor has received a draft Investiture speech from the Palace. The Prince engages in some linguistic tongue-twisters, which he finds entertaining, and his tutor berates him for his embarrassing ignorance in not knowing where the library was or about Llewelyn. And he reveals his anger that neither the previous Prince of Wales or the one before him ever turned up in Wales again.

The Prince Charles figure takes the point. He is conscientious; he visits the library and he studies.

We see the Queen and Prince Philip contemplating the Investiture speech. Here the film-makers introduce a fictional theme – that Prince Charles might adapt his own speech. We see that his parents have no confidence in him.

Back in Wales, the Prince gradually wins the sympathy of his tutor, who takes pity on him when he realises he spends the evenings alone in his room, and invites him to supper at his home. Millward's wife, rabidly hostile, is not pleased. But the Prince engages with their son and thus Millward's wife also begins to feel sorry for him. He sees a 'normal' household where people interact – a contrast to what we are urged to see as the sterile family in which he has been raised.

Prince Charles is portrayed as amiable, shy and doing his best. He learns his Welsh for the speech. The Investiture looms. His tutor says he can't bring himself to attend it for political reasons, which Prince Charles readily accepts – the tutor and his wife watch it on television in some club instead. Prince Charles apparently rewrites his speech to make it more relevant, to reflect himself and his own views, and Mountbatten turns up in his college room, dressed as an Admiral of the Fleet with Garter collar, etc. The Royal Family arrive by train, and we hear the BBC broadcast. The Queen looks angry at the reference to 'the young man who will one day succeed her'.

The real speech had touches which were Charles's – the

reference to 'a very memorable Goon' for example – but it was in no way provocative and certainly not political – as delivered here. It was approved by the Welsh Office. Nor did he hesitate over his speech as they have him do here. Listening to it, Olivia Colman plays the Queen at her most severe, while Princess Anne is portrayed as approving the rebellious element. The tutor appears to enjoy it from afar, while the crowd look bemused.

The ceremony itself is well filmed, the emphasis being a lone young man facing the world.

Prince Charles goes to say goodbye to his tutor, arriving in a chauffeur-driven Rolls-Royce, and gives him a present. The tutor wonders what his family made of the speech – he says that having delivered it in Welsh they did not understand a word of it. At the real ceremony, he did it in English and Welsh.

The film-makers ram home perceived family divisions when he gets home. The Queen is not there to greet him – she has retired to bed but agrees to see him briefly. He hopes to be thanked but no. Here the storyline goes off on its own. The Queen tells him he was sent to Wales to heal divisions, not to inflict them on his own family. The speech evidently highlighted not only the suffering of the principality but his own. The Queen reads press cuttings. He whines: 'Am I listened to in this family?'

We get a theme introduced that is explored further in later episodes – that Charles is in conflict with his family. He is the sensitive, thoughtful one. They are remote figures from another age. The Royal Family's role is to say nothing. Charles is depicted as the rebel that in real life he is not. He wants to show people who he really is. 'Mummy, we have a voice' – 'Let me let you into a secret – no one wants to hear it.'

It ends with Prince Charles delivering the 'hollow crown' speech from Shakespeare's *Richard II* in a Cambridge play – his sister, Anne, taking it all in – 'throw away tradition' being the message.

Small point – I am not sure that Marcia Williams would be sitting in the Cabinet meeting, addressed by the Duke of Norfolk.

Prince Charles's tour of Wales was a triumph. In real life, he got back to Windsor Castle to find no one to greet him. His father and sister had gone to bed, and his mother was in London with a cold. So he retreated to his room to write up his diary.

EPISODE 7

'Moondust'

This is a curious episode, with a message that emerges rather positively towards the end. It is based on the false premise that Prince Philip discovers his faith as a result of a fictitious private chat with the men who went to the moon in 1969. It depicts the plight of Prince Philip in a midlife crisis, feeling he has achieved little, is more interested in exercise and action than contemplation, and is devoid of faith (as hinted at in episode 4). By the end, he realises that there is more to life than action and achievement.

Two themes are explored to create this – the moon landings followed by the visit of the astronauts to Buckingham Palace, and the arrival of a new Dean of Windsor, Robin Woods, and the creation of what turns out to be St George's House. To achieve this, the timeline is twisted. The astronauts landed on the moon in July 1969 and visited the Palace in October 1970. The new Dean arrived at Windsor in 1962 and St George's House was opened in 1966.

The conflicting themes are banged on the head. The moon landing is a great scientific achievement (walking on 'another heavenly body'). Numerous scenes emphasise that, in contrast, Prince Philip has achieved very little, his duties are tedious and pointless, so he undergoes a spiritual awakening. At one point, he is even reckless, flying a plane to the limit of its capacity.

The moon landing part of it is an excuse for scenes of astronauts at work, the Queen sending a message to the moon, the Royal Family watching the landings, drinks in hand (the Queen Mother clutching a glass of champagne), and, in due course, the astronauts coming to London, as indeed they did on 15 October 1970, to be entertained at Buckingham Palace.

Intercut with all this are scenes involving the Dean of Windsor. The Queen is at church with a very bored Prince Philip (filmed at Englefield Church, for those who like spotting locations). The cleric is stumbling over his sermon – 'a general anaesthetic' as Prince Philip dismisses it – and he loses the plot. On the way out, the Queen suggests to Sir Michael Adeane that the Dean has reached 'the moment of his own obsolescence' after '20 years' and needs to be replaced.

That Dean was a fictional figure, but the new Dean is very real – Robin Woods, who succeeded Eric Hamilton, who died en poste in the deanery at Windsor Castle on 21 May 1962. He is rightly portrayed as a whirlwind 'with a bit of oomph'. He bounds in and talks of creating an academy or conservatoire out of empty buildings in the precincts of St George's Chapel – a place for priests in mid-life to recharge and raise their game. Prince Philip resists. He is against 'talking and thinking'. He believes you raise your game 'by action'.

It was at first hard to see how they would make good television out of this. There is a scene in which Prince Philip denigrates the 'academy' set up by the Dean. He listens to the men gathered there, musing on their chosen vocations, the dwindling congregations and a lack of interest in God, compared to some 500 million people watching the moon landings. The Dean tries to put this into perspective and then presses Prince Philip for his thoughts. His response is that what he has just heard is 'pretentious self-piteous nonsense' and that the priests should get out and do something useful. Men should make a mark. He urges action. He believes that the moon astronauts have it right whilst these priests are naval-gazing prophets of doom.

The Queen then tells Philip that there is a chance that the astronauts can come to the Palace on their victory tour. He is delighted. But the meeting will only be half an hour. Prince Philip requests some time alone with the astronauts. He is peeved to be offered only 15 minutes 'to discuss mankind's greatest achievement'.

We see him planning his questions. A lot of import is given to this private meeting. They all have colds, which give them the chance to splutter at his every inanity. Again the theme is that he has not been able to achieve what he wanted in life due to his position. As he tries to question the three men, he finds that in fact they were so busy going through the procedures that there was no time for contemplation. There is a joke about the sound of banging which turns out to be a badly working water cooler. They then ask him a lot of questions about living in a huge palace. He is gravely disappointed.

Following this depressing scene, Prince Philip visits the now empty bedroom where his mother had been housed. (She died in December 1969.)

And then we get the turnaround. He goes back to the academy, now described as St George's House (although set in a rural surrounding not inside Windsor Castle), and he talks about the three professional men with no flare or imagination. He speaks of his jealousy of the astronauts, his dedication to exercise, his dissatisfaction with his life. He speaks of his mother's death. She had seen that he missed 'faith'. He had lost his faith. Without it, what is there? 'The miracle of divine creation.' The answer is in the head or the heart, wherever faith is. 'Having ridiculed you,' he tells the gathering at St George's House that he is 'now full of respect and admiration, and not a small part of desperation.' He has come to say: 'Help! Help me.'

Having watched most of this episode with irritation, I am happy to say that, albeit in a lugubrious way and with the usual fictional examples cooked up to back their thesis, they pulled it round in the end.

In real life, Robin Woods was a splendid Dean of

Windsor. I was lucky enough to meet him when I was 14 (1966) and to see a lot of him before he moved to Worcester as their bishop in 1971, and a certain amount after that. I subscribe to the verdict in his *Times* obituary (1997) that he was the best Dean the College had in its long history. Not only did he create St George's House for the College of St George (in 1966), but also the Windsor Festival (still thriving after 50 years) and the Lay Stewards. And he did have a powerful influence on Prince Philip's religious life. Today there are more books on religion and ornithology in Prince Philip's extensive library at Buckingham Palace than on any other subject.

In a discussion I once had with Princess Anne about her grandmother, Princess Alice, she told me that her father liked to wrestle with all questions of religion. He likes to argue, and he is prepared to be swayed. I have heard him sum up many a St George's House lecture, over which he used to preside. He has explored not only Christianity but also many other religions and he has seen many far-off places where these religions are followed.

At the end of the episode, the captions tell us that Prince Philip and the Dean became 'lifelong friends' – 'For over 50 years St George's House has been a centre for the exploration of faith and philosophy ... Its success is the achievement of which Philip is perhaps most proud.'

I ended this episode thinking that perhaps this is the best publicity St George's House will have had in its

53-year history. And I wonder if it will be shown there and discussed.

Small points – Robin Woods was born in 1914, so he was not the same age as Prince Philip, who was born in 1921. The Queen would not have 'an audience with the astronauts'; she would receive them, as she did. The Duke of Gloucester is still up and about!

On the plus side, unexplained, there is an amusing vignette of the ebullient amateur astrologer Patrick Moore as the television studio guest during the moon landings.

EPISODE 8

'Dangling Man'

The Duke of Windsor is the focus of this episode and the theme explored is the one generally perceived to be at the core of the Abdication – the path of love versus that of duty. The time frame is late 1970 until May 1972, but well-known events are out of sequence. They are considerably jumbled in order to suit the chosen thesis.

The Duke of Windsor, now played by Derek Jacobi instead of Alex Jennings, is ill. *The Crown* likes illness – so we get the Duke spluttering with throat cancer, similar to the opening scenes in the first episode when George VI was vomiting. He too vomits. This is 1970. (He was not ill until 1971.) At the American Hospital, the Windsors are told that the Duke is terminally ill (they were not told – he said, even close to the end, that he was not ill but that it was the cortisone that made him feel so bad). She tells the Duke they must throw a party.

The Windsors are visited, as indeed they were, in October

1971, by Emperor Hirohito of Japan, whom the Duke had first met when he visited London in 1921, and Empress Nagako. According to the film, the Duke sees this late life visit as the last chance to restore his reputation. So he fixes for cameras to be there. The Emperor resents this as he does not want to be photographed with a man who lost his throne. In real life, the Emperor and Empress posed happily with the Windsors but on the terrace, not in the drawing room. The film-makers still give the Duke almost Shakespearian lines as he muses on living on an island where he had once reigned as Sovereign.

The Emperor's conciliatory visit appears to annoy the Queen and in particular the Queen Mother, as does the idea that the Duke is about to give an interview about his life to the BBC, which was in fact filmed two years before in late 1969 and shown on television in January 1970. The Queen refers to the Queen Mother's loathing of the Windsors. (Actually she had been very fond of the Duke, and took the line that she did not know the Duchess and therefore could not hate her.) The Queen announces that she has given Prince Charles permission to visit the Duke (which he did, when staying with the Ambassador, Christopher Soames, at the British Embassy on 3 October 1971). In this episode he arrives alone, whereas his real-life visit was in the evening and there were other guests present.

A new theme is introduced. Camilla Shand is dating Andrew Parker Bowles. Meeting him in a pub, she berates him for an affair he has had, and goes off with a miscellaneous young man instead of accompanying him to a ball, which gives an idea of what we are meant to make of their relationship. Parker Bowles is on the loose, goes to the ball and meets Princess Anne. She comes on to him; she has been watching him on the polo field. (There are photos of them both at polo matches at Windsor and it seems they saw a lot of each other between 1969 and 1971 or so.) However, unless things have changed a great deal these days, the scene that follows might, I suggest, require some scrutiny from her lawyers. In the course of it, the Parker Bowles character warns her, in nautical metaphors, that there is another figure on the scene – Camilla. The film-makers tell us their impression of the nature of the relationship between Parker Bowles and Princess Anne, deeming it somewhat casual.

The next scene shows Prince Charles playing polo, watched by the Queen Mother and Mountbatten (who, in real life, had no rapport whatsoever). Prince Charles and Mountbatten then meet for a meal. They discuss the Duke and Duchess of Windsor, somewhat disparagingly. Prince Charles tells his great-uncle that he and the Duke have been writing to each other (which, up to a point, they did, though the Duke certainly never interfered with his private life – nor advised him to get a wife). Mountbatten tells him to sow his wild oats, play the field. This advice was given in a letter to the real Prince Charles in 1974:

> I believe, in a case like yours, the man should sow his wild
> oats and have as many affairs as he can before settling
> down but for a wife he should choose a suitable, attractive
> and sweet-charactered girl *before* she met anyone else she
> might fall for ...

Prince Charles reveals that he has met the young Camilla
Shand and is much taken with her. He claims that she
used to be with Parker Bowles but they fell out over his
sister Anne. He wants to 'snap' Camilla 'up'. Mountbatten
is non-committal.

It would seem that Prince Charles met Camilla some
time in 1971, and that they became particularly close
towards the latter part of 1972, therefore after the death
of the Duke of Windsor. He calls Camilla and invites her
to dinner. There is some telephonic flirting. The timeline is deeply muddled in the next few scenes. Heath
becomes Prime Minister (June 1970). This leads to discussion between the Queen and Prince Philip about a
state visit to France (May 1972). Martin Charteris is now
the Private Secretary (he took over in January 1972). He
tells the Queen about the Duke of Windsor's forthcoming TV interview (January 1970) but proposes a visit to
him, which eventually took place in May 1972. Prince
Philip says 'certainly not'. Charteris refers to the successful visit of Emperor Hirohito (in October 1971). He asks
why if the Japanese visit the Duke, his own family does
not. (Heath suggested that to Robert Armstrong on 7

November 1971 – see Hugo Vickers, *Behind Closed Doors* (2011), page 15.)

A car arrives at the Palace (through the front gates as always in this series, whereas only for the great ceremonies in real life). Camilla comes to dinner with the Prince – he talks of his life as a predicament. He is a tortured soul. He dreads his mother's death and yet he desires to be King. It is not for me to probe his mind, but my understanding is that the real Prince Charles has long considered his main contribution to public life is as Prince of Wales and he is in no hurry to assume the burdens of kingship.

We get a Saul Bellow reference to show that the Prince is a reader, whereas his dinner guest has never heard of him. The book was *Dangling Man* (1944) – in which the hero exists in a kind of ridiculous abyss (an unemployed man in Chicago, waiting to be drafted in World War II, to give some meaning to his life). Then there is a joke exploding letter to show their shared childish humour. Suddenly the interview with the Duke of Windsor is to begin, so back we go to January 1970, before they had met.

The Windsors appear (with Kenneth Harris). The Duke's message is that he had wanted to do things his way and that when he acceded, he continued in that vein. He claims that the real reason they wanted to get rid of him was not so much his wish to marry the Duchess but because of his independence. We see his family watching independently – the Queen interested but concerned, Prince Philip hating them, the Queen Mother dismissive and disdainful, and Lord Mountbatten shrugging. But Prince Charles watches in wonderment.

Princess Anne saunters along the corridor. Her summation of the Parker Bowleses is: 'Just make sure things remain the right way round. Us playing with Camilla and Andrew – not them playing with us.'

Seemingly it is 1972 again. The Duke of Windsor is spluttering over a letter to Prince Charles. The doctor comes. Later he retreats from the bridge table, again ill. He is put on a drip and lies in his bed. The Queen arrives on her state visit, arriving (curiously) first in Rouen, on her state visit to President Pompidou, which heralds Britain's entry into the Common Market.

Then they go to Paris. Martin Charteris tells the Queen that there is a message – the Duke of Windsor is close to the end. Spontaneously she decides to visit him, taking everyone by surprise. Sidney, the Bahamian butler, comes to the bedroom and announces she is on her way. In reality, the visit had long been planned for 18 May, on her way back from the races. Indeed, Sir Christopher Soames, the British Ambassador, was anxious that the Duke should not die during or just before the state visit.

The Queen is alone (the Duke of Edinburgh and Prince Charles were with her in reality). She looks with disapproval at a box in the hall, marked 'THE KING'. For some reason, it bears the Prince of Wales's feathers.

The Duke has risen from his bed and is dressed. When the Queen comes into the Duke's room, he is attached to drips by nurses and seated in a wheelchair. He rises from it with difficulty, which in reality he did. She tells him he was always her favourite uncle. Having begun with 'Your Majesty', he then calls her 'Lilibet', as he would have done. She responds 'Shirley Temple' – a nickname he had used for her, not that she would refer to it in real life.

His speech to her involves him saying: 'I underestimated you. The Crown always finds its way to the right head: my father, my brother and you.' There is then a discussion about Prince Charles, the Duke telling her that she does not think him up for it – which she denies saying. His message is 'with the right woman by his side, he will make a good King'.

He goes on about Camilla – which he could not have done as they were not close by then. And I am sure there were no letters about her. Nevertheless, the Queen takes them. He apologises: 'Forgive me.' The Queen replies: 'Thank you. What you did. Your Abdication of the throne did change my life forever … There are days when I consider it to be a blessing. I've even on occasions found myself wanting to thank you.' In reality, the Duke of Windsor never felt the need to ask forgiveness from anybody for abdicating. And the Queen accepted her lot, though it is well known that the Royal Family attributed some blame to the Duke for the early death of his brother, George VI, on whose shoulders he landed so many responsibilities.

The Queen holds his hand. Unlike with Churchill in

episode 1, when the Duke proceeds to lose consciousness, she does not kiss him. She walks slowly out.

There is a flashback to Prince Charles writing to the Duke about the nature of kingship and of love. He says he recognises himself in the Duke, which I am quite sure he did not. He seems to be thinking that the Duke should have stayed as King with Wallis at his side. He promises he will not be denied what he has been denied. Again, this fundamentally undermines Prince Charles's approach to his role as Prince of Wales.

Then we see the Duchess holding the Duke's hand. His pug suddenly jumps from the bed. It is true that his dog did leave the bed shortly before his death, as dogs sometimes do. He dies. The Duchess looks distraught as the nurse leads her from the bedside. In fact, the Duke did not want her to see him in extremis as he wished to spare her suffering. She was asleep in her own bed when he died in the night of 28 May 1972.

EPISODE 9

'Imbroglio'

One of the suggestions of this episode is to suggest that Lord Mountbatten and the Queen Mother plotted against Prince Charles to prevent his evident decision to marry Camilla Shand in 1972. The Duke of Windsor's death is to the fore in the opening scenes, so we are at the end of May 1972. We see the coffin arriving, draped in a full royal standard (without his particular label – three points, the centre one bearing a crown) so the film-makers have inadvertently reinvented him as King.

Next is the burial, with the Duchess of Windsor at the graveside, where Garter King of Arms reads out his styles and titles (this did happen, but in St George's Chapel). At the reception, the Duchess gives Prince Charles the Duke's pocket watch, with the Queen and the Queen Mother looking on disapprovingly. The Duchess seems to know about Camilla and gives him two bits of advice. The first is: 'Never turn your back on true love, despite all the

49

sacrifices. David and I never once regretted it.' The second is: 'Watch out for your family.' He says: 'They mean well.' – 'No they don't,' says the Duchess. We see her leaving all alone.

It is perhaps worth stating that the Duchess of Windsor never wanted the Duke to abdicate. Though they could never admit that they regretted the Abdication, I fear they did. I only ever saw him once but I have never seen a man with sadder eyes.

We then cut to a scene of questionable taste, Prince Charles, partly naked, in bed with Camilla, expressing his admiration for his recently deceased great-uncle. He thinks they united against him because he was brighter, wittier and more independent of thought. This is a recurring theme of this season – the Royal Family's cold dedication to duty, at the cost of warm human relations. He thinks he is the new pariah.

The facts do not support the portrayed scene. The Duchess of Windsor was appreciative of Prince Charles's kindness to her. He was sympathetic, called her Aunt Wallis, and had sought to effect a reconciliation between the ailing Windsors and his family. The Queen Mother had not supported this. Prince Charles and Lord Mountbatten had joined the Duchess when she came down from London to see the Duke's Lying-in-State, but she was already unwell and in no state to give Prince Charles advice about his love life, nor would she see it as her place to do so. She was not well at the funeral, and soon afterwards her health collapsed and she entered the long illness which finally ended with her death in 1986.

The episode moves on to Edward Heath, a flashback to his childhood and a piano his family cannot afford, the miners' strike of 1974, power cuts and the three-day week, a theme which recurs again in this episode. But suddenly we go back to the Silver Wedding of 1972.

Prince Charles is in the Navy, being trained and lonely on the high seas. He relates this to Camilla over the telephone but she is confused, as well she might be since we observe the hovering presence of Andrew Parker Bowles.

Mountbatten arrives somewhere (filmed at Greenwich). Charles bemoans his plight to his great-uncle, who only sees Camilla as a bit of fun. He pleads for his help. But Dickie is not on his side over this one. He throws in his hand with the Queen Mother to scupper the Charles–Camilla affair. This is of course incredible to anyone with any knowledge of the complete lack of empathy between the Queen Mother and Mountbatten. She was able to get her way quietly over many things and was suspicious of his meddling. So, as the plotline veers once more into the realms of fantasy, we hear that Mountbatten will have Charles posted overseas for eight months, while the Queen Mother agrees to take on the Shand and Parker Bowles families.

There is an interlude with Heath and a piece of coal in cabinet to remind him of the miners. Heath confronts the leader of the N.U.M. Heath is impressive on the subject of democracy. So back to 1974.

The Queen Mother then activates the Shands, parents of Camilla, and the Parker Bowleses, parents of Andrew, pressing for a marriage between them. Charles goes to see the Queen and is told that he is to be stationed in the Caribbean for eight months. In reality, Prince Charles was not sent to the Caribbean in order to separate him from Camilla. He mentions perhaps it is because Camilla is not 'intact'. The Queen summons Lord Mountbatten and the Queen Mother as if they were recalcitrant schoolchildren. The Queen seems to be promoting the idea of Camilla. She does not know about the Parker Bowles link. Princess Anne arrives home in her car, listening to pop music. (She is so well played, that however absurd the plot, it is enjoyable whenever she appears.)

The episode continues with talk of 'true love', Princess Anne being confronted by the Queen, Prince Philip, the Queen Mother and Lord Mountbatten. She tells them that Camilla is obsessed with Andrew Parker Bowles, that she herself was briefly caught up in all this but that it was just 'a bit of fun'. If Charles went forward with Camilla there would be 'three in the marriage'.

Mountbatten delivers the bad news to Prince Charles, who crumples up. He talks to Camilla. Her line is that yes, she loves Andrew, and apparently it will be better for everyone in the long run. In real life, Prince Charles heard about it while serving overseas, so all this was melodrama.

Politically, Heath is in trouble. The country is in trouble. The Queen is cross about the miners' strike, so this is 1974.

We revert to the Queen's Silver Wedding in 1972, seeing an evening occasion with the Lord Mayor, Prince Philip wearing the Order of Merit now (correctly). As the Queen speaks of happy family values, we get a glimpse of the lonely Prince Charles at sea, looking at the inscription on his pocket watch, and the Duchess of Windsor, a lonely widow in Paris. We cut to the Queen Mother at the wedding of Andrew Parker Bowles and Camilla, smiling smugly. Prince Charles weeps pathetically – in the Caribbean.

Much has been written about the Charles–Camilla relationship. To recap, they met in 1971. Mountbatten made them welcome at Broadlands and encouraged Charles to sow his wild oats. He did not imagine that Charles should marry Camilla. Prince Charles entered the Royal Navy and went off to sea in January 1973. While serving overseas, he heard that Camilla had married Andrew Parker Bowles. The engagement was announced on 15 March 1973. That wedding took place at the Guards' Chapel on 4 July 1973, in the presence of the Queen Mother (an old friend of the groom's parents), Princess Anne and Princess Margaret.

It is accepted that at that time Camilla was in love with Andrew Parker Bowles, a good-looking cavalry officer, who knew when to strike. Meanwhile the young Prince of Wales was too unsure of himself to make up his mind. There was no need for any Palace plot.

'Cri de Coeur'

The last episode in this series concentrates on the break-up of Princess Margaret's marriage to Lord Snowdon. The Queen visits Princess Margaret, who is in bed. There has been a marital row. There is evidence of Snowdon's infidelity. 'He can't help himself, my priapic little snapper.' The girl in question turns out to be Lucy Lindsay-Hogg, spotted by Lady Glenconner, who tells Princess Margaret this at a party, which she attends alone.

At a dinner, the Queen explains that Wilson is back – so it would appear to be March 1974. Yet it is also Princess Margaret's birthday party so 21 August 1974. The Duke of Gloucester is at the table, despite having died on 10 June. Princess Margaret declares that Snowdon is now openly unfaithful and wants him banned. The family praise Snowdon's various talents. Princess Margaret storms out.

Lady Glenconner invites Princess Margaret to stay with her at Glen, the Tennant castle in Scotland. On the way there, one of Snowdon's nasty messages to her is found tucked into a book. According to Anne Glenconner's best-selling memoirs, *Lady in Waiting* (2019), such messages were delivered. Scenes at Glen bear some resemblance to her version in that book – likewise those in Mustique.

Princess Margaret travels by train – in the kind of bed I have never seen on a train – and then a huge Rolls-Royce conveys her to Glen. She arrives asleep. Actually she didn't – she was collected and by the time she arrived, Roddy Llewellyn was in the car. In this film, Lady Glenconner produces Roddy beside the swimming pool and a relationship develops. Peebles, where they go shopping, looks more like Berkshire than Scotland.

There are scenes at Glen and on Mustique which encapsulate this relationship, but no, a bearded press photographer did not find his way onto Mustique and take snaps of Roddy rubbing sun cream into Princess Margaret's legs. (Perhaps they muddled this up with Fergie and John Bryan in 1992?)

Lord Snowdon visits the Queen to show her some Silver Jubilee commemoratives he has designed, so it seems we are now in 1976. Whether the Queen lectured him about the state of his marriage is more questionable. In this conversation, he sidesteps any blame and cites the presence of Roddy. Nor did the Queen Mother summon Princess Margaret back from Mustique – that was not her style. Clearly the delight shown by Lucy Lindsay-Hogg in finally nailing the marriage is highly speculative – as if she were the Machiavellian provocateur in the separation. She provokes Snowdon in his darkroom.

Princess Margaret did not return to find Snowdon ensconced in Kensington Palace as shown here. In real life, he was in Australia when the separation was announced (March 1976) and had already debunked to his mother's house.

There is a political subplot. Wilson has returned after the 1974 election but now, two years on, he admits to Alzheimer's. He tells the Queen he is resigning. Quite out of character, the Queen tells him: 'I don't mind admitting I let out an unconstitutional cheer when you beat Mr Heath this time.' Wilson tells her: 'Look what a sentimental old Royalist I turned out to be.'

There is truth in that – there had been some concern when Wilson arrived as Prime Minister, but in the end he caused no trouble. The Queen tells him that she and Prince Philip would like to dine with him at Downing Street. They did do that.

Hardly has he left than the Queen is told that Princess Margaret has taken an overdose. She did take an overdose, though not on this occasion. It happened after she had been staying in a commune with Roddy and he fled to Turkey to get away from her (more likely 1978). The Queen Mother describes this as 'a cri de coeur rather than a coup de grace'. Lord Napier later told the biographer, Tim Heald that he thought the overdose was probably done to create a drama: 'Remember she was a great actress.'

When the Queen visits her again, Princess Margaret tells her she and Tony will eventually divorce – the first royal divorce since Henry VIII and Anne of Cleves. What about Lord Harewood, son of the Princess Royal, in 1967? The Queen says they can time the announcement of the separation to coincide with Wilson's resignation (March 1976). Those two events did coincide.

There follows one of the better discussions in the series – Princess Margaret reassuring the Queen about the Silver Jubilee, the Queen suggesting that in 25 years she has achieved nothing and the country has declined while Princess Margaret tells her that she has bestowed calm on the nation. She suggests that what the monarchy does is nothing more than 'paper over the cracks' – a slightly dismal verdict.

One small change from reality on the day of the Silver Jubilee – as the Gold State Coach leaves, they make Prince Philip ride behind it, whereas, in real life, he was seated beside the Queen in the coach. I guess they wanted her symbolically alone.

While attention has been paid to uniforms, orders and decorations in this series, the Duke of Kent (briefly spotted in the royal line-up) is missing his GCMG collar.

The last scene shows the Queen alone in her coach on the way to the Silver Jubilee service at St Paul's Cathedral. As viewers will have come to expect in this series, Olivia Colman plays her as sullen and glum, the message being that she has to carry on, whether she has done it right or wrong – again a depressing verdict. But it backs up Princess Margaret's statement: 'The rest of us drop like flies, but she goes on and on.'

Finally, it was good to see them resurrecting the late Duke of Gloucester again. I was getting used to his post-humous appearances. There he was, correctly placed in order of precedence, below Princess Margaret, but before his wife and before the Duke of Kent. He was dressed not in his Scots Guards uniform, but in a morning coat, splen-didly adorned with his Garter star, medals and a Garter collar.

Good of them to take so much trouble to dress him up. By then he had been dead for three years.

SEASON 1

The first ten episodes of *The Crow*n
were released on 4 November 2016.

EPISODE I

'Wolferton Splash'

The series opens with King George VI spewing blood into a lavatory pan, to indicate that he is a sick man. Before the opening credits, there is a scene in which the King invests Prince Philip as Duke of Edinburgh. Prince Philip is described as a Prince of Greece and 'of' Denmark. Then the King knights him as he bestows titles on him in the wrong order, and only afterwards gives him the Order of the Garter. There is a scene in which the King uses the 'C' word. We are introduced to the Prince Philip character, smoking a cigarette on the day before the wedding and treating it all as something of a game.

This episode introduces the various themes. We see tension between the King and Prince Philip; we meet Group Captain Peter Townsend hovering amorously around Princess Margaret, and Princess Elizabeth preparing for her future role, at work with her father.

At the 1947 royal wedding, Prince Philip's mother is

depicted in a nun's habit – in reality she was a civilian then and did not adopt the habit (which she wore at the Coronation) until 1948. But this allows Queen Elizabeth (the Queen Mother) to describe her disparagingly as 'the hun nun'. But then she calls her daughter 'Elizabeth' when it was always 'Lilibet'. There are scenes of Princess Elizabeth's carefree life in Malta, though her son, Prince Charles, was not in Malta at that time.

The King has to have an operation, so we see Princess Margaret waiting anxiously with Queen Mary while the King is with his doctors. There are gory scenes of the lung being removed and then wrapped up in a copy of *The Times* (a story gleaned from Hugh Trevor-Roper's letters). There is a moment where Sir John Weir, the well-known homeopathic doctor, informs the King of the gravity of his illness even after the operation. It is curious that this role was assigned to Weir. In reality he failed to give the King proper advice. He was even mistrusted by the admirable Dr Margery Blackie, the most distinguished of homeopathic doctors, who had little time for him.

In 1948 Dermot Morrah, respected *Times* writer, reported privately that the King was in danger of losing his leg: 'One special source of anxiety is his personal physician – a homeopathic quack with a fascination for women, some of whom planted him on Edward, Prince of Wales, who bequeathed him to his successor as official medical officer. Of course they've called in good men as consultants, Cassidy and Learmouth especially, but this old menace is there all the time, and it was he who let the trouble go to this length before sounding the alarm.'

It was just as bad in 1951, in which this episode is set. Weir accompanied the King to Balmoral for the summer. The worldly doctor enjoyed himself shooting with Scottish dukes. Only when the local doctor was called in was the gravity of the King's illness appreciated, resulting in him being whisked down to London to have his lung removed. Following that, those who understood such things realised that the King's life was likely to be short.

This episode depicts Churchill becoming Prime Minister again (in October 1951), and suggests that neither he nor the King are in good health. The King is forced to wear rouge (which was the case). In reality it is not certain how much the King was told about his state of health. The episode ends with Princess Elizabeth looking at the King's boxes, and in a sense facing her destiny.

Minor mistakes – Princess Elizabeth's car has the royal coat of arms on it, which is reserved for the monarch; Lady Churchill's GBE riband at the wedding is too red and too wide.

EPISODE 2

'Hyde Park Corner'

Episode 1 warned us that the King's life was in danger. Episode 2 carries him off. It starts with Princess Elizabeth arriving in Kenya on the first leg of the proposed Commonwealth tour she is undertaking on her father's behalf.

We see the royal limousine arriving at an event and the Royal Standard fluttering on the front of it, the inference here being that Princess Elizabeth has already become Queen – but no, it is the wrong Royal Standard. Princess Elizabeth's would have had a label of three white points. Soon afterwards a cocky Prince Philip mocks a Kikuyu chieftain for wearing a medal to which he is apparently not entitled (in fact a Victoria Cross, though this is not explained). This was in February 1952, and yet Prince Philip was wearing a 1953 Coronation medal. Arguably this might not have mattered, but for the fact that he was chiding someone else for wearing the wrong medal.

As they arrive at Treetops for the fateful night of 5/6 February, the Prince Philip character does a *Crocodile Dundee* feat in seeing off a bull elephant. In reality there were no elephants there that day or night.

The scenes in which Lord Salisbury is seen plotting to get rid of Churchill have not been well received by the Cecil family due to inaccuracies. He would never have elicited the help of Lord Mountbatten, for example. Anthony Eden did not go to Sandringham to ask the King to exercise his constitutional right to remove the Prime Minister from office on account of his incapacity to run the country properly, least of all in February 1952. Churchill himself is given a fictitious secretary called Venetia Scott, so that she can play a role in episode 4.

Following the King's death, we see a gruesome scene in which Princess Margaret visits the body of her father during the embalming process. Churchill did not broadcast in the presence of the entire Cabinet, yet his actual words are as moving to listen to today as they surely were at the time. Tommy Lascelles, the Private Secretary, is invested with a most sinister role. He is given good lines, such as when he passes on the Queen Mother's offer to Townsend to become her Comptroller at Clarence House: 'I don't expect you to accept.'

Minor mistakes – it was not Lascelles who told Churchill of the King's death, it was Sir Edward Ford; Queen Mary was told by Lady Cynthia Colville, not by a footman; it is unlikely that Princess Elizabeth had just written to her father before hearing of his death; Queen Mary did not come to Sandringham to curtsey to the new Queen (that happened at Clarence House); there is nothing to suggest that Lascelles caught Princess Margaret and Townsend kissing; contemporary evidence proves that the Queen Mother did not cry hysterically when she heard of the King's death (she was far too stoical); Martin Charteris did not disappear from royal service immediately after the King's death (he became part of the team, though no longer the new Queen's actual Private Secretary). Some of these things are acceptable under the heading of dramatic licence.

EPISODE 3

'Windsor'

Back we go to 1936, seeing Princess Elizabeth and Princess Margaret playing just before their uncle, King Edward VIII, broadcasts his Abdication speech. There is no way that Queen Mary would have come into the room to see the King and try to dissuade him from broadcasting. And Mrs Simpson was not hovering in the background as he made that speech. In reality she was in Cannes. In the real Abdication speech he was announced as 'His Royal Highness Prince Edward', not as Duke of Windsor.

Presently there are many scenes involved with the aftermath of King George VI's death: the young Queen wearing black and sometimes a black veil, and Tommy Lascelles becoming ever more the dominant figure in the Palace.

Two big issues are explored to show how Prince Philip no longer has any say in the running of his family. There are many scenes of the redecoration of Clarence House under his direction. He wants the family to stay there. He insists that the Queen puts this proposal to Churchill. It is understood that, in real life, the Queen and Prince Philip would have preferred to stay at Clarence House, which was the perfect London home for a young family, not too big, and with a well-sized garden. Buckingham Palace has always served multiple purposes: a series of state rooms, offices for members of the Household, and the King's and Queen's rooms along a long corridor on the Constitution Hill side. It must have been a bit like living in an Edwardian hotel. But Churchill insisted that the monarch must live in the Palace, and so they moved in on 5 May 1952. The Queen Mother stayed on, only moving into Clarence House on 18 May 1953.

The other issue is the family name. This was another genuine cause for Prince Philip to be upset. In this episode, Lord Mountbatten, curiously dressed for dinner as an Admiral in his own home (Broadlands), boasts, with some justification, that the House of Mountbatten now reigns in Britain. Normally the male who marries a Queen Regnant gives his name to the new house; hence Queen Victoria was the last Queen of the House of Hanover, which became Saxe-Coburg when she married Prince Albert in 1840. Prince Ernst August of Hanover was at Mountbatten's table in 1952 and did not like what he heard. He informed Queen Mary, who called for Jock Colville, then Private Secretary to Winston Churchill. The Prime Minister duly informed the Queen that the Royal House must be called the House of Windsor. There is a fictional scene in which the Queen reads out this declaration to the Privy Council.

It is true that Prince Philip was livid about this, though in reality he wanted it called the House of Edinburgh, rather than Mountbatten, the preferred choice of his ever-manipulative uncle. Harold Macmillan recorded that Prince Philip wrote a well-reasoned memorandum making his case, but the Government would not countenance the Mountbatten name being used. In opposing Prince Philip, ministers such as Macmillan were keen to send 'a shot across his bows', to keep the young consort in his place.

The Duke of Windsor comes over for his brother's funeral, and the series makes much of the newly-styled Queen Mother's hostility to him. The Duke of Windsor also wants various things. There is a lot of bargaining in this episode. The Queen asks Churchill to do her a favour by informing the Cabinet about the Mountbatten name, claiming that she is keeping him in office by agreeing to a delayed Coronation. In fact the Coronation was always planned for June 1953, as it takes a long time to arrange such a ceremony.

Then Churchill asks the Duke of Windsor to be an intermediary with the Queen for the other two issues of this episode: the family name and the move to Buckingham Palace. In exchange, the Duke wants to retain the allowance King George VI promised him (which ceased at the King's death), and again demands an HRH for the

Duchess. There is a curious scene in which three contrasting aspects of love are explored: we see a sequence with the Windsors dancing romantically, the Queen and Prince Philip at the opera (where he takes her hand), and Princess Margaret popping into Townsend's office to kiss him with some passion.

The Duke of Windsor then lunches with the Queen, which did not happen in real life, and puts Churchill's two points to her. Most erroneously, we find the young new Queen turning to the Duke of Windsor for avuncular advice. He is presented as a sage, and explains, in the almost Shakespearian language the scriptwriters give him, why she, as a monarch, must move from Clarence House to Buckingham Palace.

Alex Jennings, the actor, looks incredibly like the Duke of Windsor, but the real life Duke never delivered such Shakespearian oratory. Nor would the real Queen ever have asked for advice from a man so patently incapable of giving it.

The Duke of Windsor had been immensely tiresome ever since the Abdication in 1936, and Tommy Lascelles had seen him off on more than one occasion, most effectively in 1945. The Royal Family felt gravely let down by the Abdication, and Lascelles wrote at one point in the 1940s that any appearance in Britain by the Duke would have a grave effect on the health and peace of mind of George VI. Later on, in real life, the Queen was considerate to her uncle, and various rapprochements were made before he died. But the trouble with the Duke of Windsor was that if he was given an inch, he would take a mile.

In other themes, we see Prince Philip asking Group Captain Townsend to teach him to fly, a theme followed up in the next episode. He did learn at White Waltham, near Maidenhead, but was taught by Flight Lieutenant C.R. Gordon, of Cheltenham. He received his wings from Air Chief Marshal Sir William Dickson, on 4 May 1953, having flown for 90 to 100 hours.

The film-makers also introduce the idea that Prince Philip bullied Prince Charles, which is again addressed in later episodes.

Minor mistakes – Prince Philip was a descendant of the royal houses of Greece and Denmark, but not of Norway. King Haakon of Norway (1872-1957) was a Prince of Denmark who was given the Norwegian throne in 1905.

A recurring mistake throughout the series: all the characters arrive at Buckingham Palace through the ceremonial front gates. Normally they enter via the gate to the right near Constitution Hill.

EPISODE 4

'Act of God'

This is a curious episode based on the great fog that descended on London between 5 and 9 December 1952. This fog encouraged some spontaneous burglaries and one murder. London was perfectly used to fogs, so it was not treated as a particular emergency until much later, when it was estimated that between 4,000 and 12,000 people died – though most of them had breathing problems or were very old. Most of this episode is fantastical and did not happen. Obviously the scenes involving Churchill's fictional secretary, Venetia Scott, were made up. She is killed when hit by a bus due to the fog. Since there was no public transport working, other than trains on the London Underground, this could not have happened.

The film-makers then introduce Churchill failing to take action; the question of Clement Attlee, the Leader of the Opposition, potentially turning the situation to political advantage; and Churchill's decision to visit a hospital during the crisis. All this is fiction too. Interestingly, the fog did not rate a mention in Martin Gilbert's official biography of Churchill.

The other scenes involve Prince Philip learning to fly and Government annoyance at this. Queen Mary falls ill and takes to her bed, attended by Sir John Weir. The Queen walks through the fog to visit her ailing grandmother to discuss what is expected of her as a monarch.

EPISODE 5

'Smoking Mirrors – Crowning The Queen'

There is a flashback to 11 May, with George VI explaining the significance of anointing in the Coronation ceremony, and talking of the weight of the crown, both actual and symbolic. The action then moves forward to 1953, with the Queen trying on the same crown before her Coronation.

Queen Mary falls gravely ill, which brings the Duke of Windsor over. In this series he comes from France, though he actually came with his sister, the Princess Royal, from New York. There are lots of opportunities for him to complain to the Duchess of Windsor about his family, his mother, and his treatment. The Queen is warned by the Queen Mother to be wary of the Duke: 'Like mercury, he'll slip through the tiniest crack.' During his visit, the Duke is summoned from Marlborough House to Lambeth Palace, where he finds the Archbishop of Canterbury, Tommy Lascelles, and one other, ranged against him explaining why he should not attend the Coronation and why the Duchess would not be invited. The Duke is furious, but he agrees to put out a statement explaining why he won't be there.

While he is at Lambeth Palace, a message comes through that Queen Mary has died. In reality the Duke was not at Lambeth Palace. Her funeral is shown (with the Royal Standard on her coffin, not her personal standard).

In real life, the question of the Duke's possible attendance at the Coronation preoccupied the Archbishop of Canterbury as early as November 1952, and he raised the matter with the Queen at lunch. It was agreed that his presence 'would create a very difficult situation for everybody, and if he had not the wits to see that for himself, then he ought to be told it.' Churchill took the line that while it was understandable that the Duke would wish to be present at family funerals, it would be completely inappropriate for him to attend the Coronation of one of his successors. Tommy Lascelles wrote to the Duke's lawyers, making it clear that no summons would be forthcoming. A statement was prepared for the Duke to issue to save face, but he must have alarmed the British Government by giving an interview at Cherbourg in which he said he might well be in England at the time of the ceremony. As it happened, he and the Duchess stayed in Paris and watched it on television with friends, a scene recreated in this episode. We see the Duke explaining the proceedings in the Abbey, again in Shakespearian phrases, to a group of undistinguished guests. The episode ends with him playing his bagpipes outside the house, with tears in his eyes, presumably to hint that he is regretting all that he discarded.

The other main theme in this episode is the role of Prince Philip in the preparations, and also in respect of the part he intends to play in the ceremony. Here he only agrees to chair the Coronation Committee if he has total control, and we see him coming out with all sorts of modern ideas for the day, such as inviting Trade Union leaders and businessmen to take part. He is told that some things cannot be changed. There is a row with the Queen and he tells her he refuses to kneel before her to do homage. In the end he is obliged to do so, but he is given credit for insisting the ceremony be televised.

Having written a book on the Coronation and delved into the Archbishop of Canterbury's papers, I can testify that these reveal the Archbishop of Canterbury pushing Prince Philip out as much as possible. He pronounced: 'There must be no association of him in any way with the process & rite of Coronation.' Yet they also show that Prince Philip was quite happy to do fealty after the Archbishop (when he could have been expected to go first), and that he presented a silver gilt wafer box to the Abbey, and a chalice and paten to Lambeth, as a form of offering to respect taking his place next to the Queen during the communion.

Unlike other flaky consorts, such as Prince Claus of the Netherlands and Prince Henrik of Denmark, Prince

Philip was raised within the Royal House of Greece. But for the birth of the future King Constantine in 1940, he would have ended up as King of Greece in 1964, and marriage with Princess Elizabeth would have been out of the question. In real life he adapted quickly to his changed circumstances, but in *The Crown*, they put him in conflict at every opportunity.

The Coronation was a wonderful opportunity to create a scene of great visual magnificence, but it fell seriously short in regard to a great number of details. Earl Mountbatten, seated in the front row of the Royal Box (he was not in the front row) appears dressed in ducal robes, and is not wearing his Garter collar. Nor is the supporting actor representing the Queen's uncle, the Duke of Gloucester. The Marquess of Salisbury carries the Sword of State (which he did at the actual Coronation), but he crowns himself with an Earl's coronet. The Dowager Duchess of Devonshire (Mistress of the Robes) fails to put on a coronet. The oath was not administered during the anointing, but before it. There are a number of Peeresses sitting where the Peers sat in reality. Thus this important scene proves disappointing.

The St Edward's Crown with which the Queen is crowned is far too big, but this may have been intentional, to demonstrate the burden the Queen was assuming.

EPISODE 6

'Gelignite'

The theme of this episode is the Princess Margaret/Peter Townsend love affair and their attempt to marry in 1953. The opening scene shows the Queen and Prince Philip going to the Coronation Derby, but we then see a newspaper office where an unshaven journalist has picked up what he realises is a huge scoop (hence 'gelignite'): Princess Margaret having been observed picking some fluff off the jacket of Group Captain Peter Townsend at the Coronation – he being by then a divorced equerry. Princess Margaret and Townsend are on the point of accompanying the Queen Mother on an official visit to Rhodesia.

The Princess invites the Queen and Prince Philip to dine with her and Townsend, and they believe that they have her blessing, but they soon run up against the establishment. Tommy Lascelles invokes the Royal Marriages Act of 1772, which stated that no lineal descendant of George II could marry without the consent of the Sovereign, and so

Princess Margaret is asked to wait for two years. The series suggests that the Queen deceived her sister by appearing to support her wish to marry him and then eventually forbidding it. The film-makers imply that the Princess never forgave her sister, a theme which recurs in later episodes. The sequence of events is somewhat muddled. Since there are also a number of contradictory accounts left by Peter Townsend, Tommy Lascelles, and Princess Margaret to her biographer, it is hard to settle on a true version, since that true version depends on which source is trusted.

Lascelles appears at his most severe in this episode, a Satanic and menacing figure. This is an interpretation that might well have resonated with the real life Princess Margaret, not to mention the real life Peter Townsend.

There is no doubt that Princess Margaret fell in love with the Group Captain. He was the trusted equerry of the father she adored and a Battle of Britain hero. He was rather a gentle figure. However, as Lascelles made clear to him in no uncertain terms, he had been placed in a position of trust and responsibility. He was a married man with two sons and he was considerably older than the Princess. The real Lascelles said of him: 'He has Theudas trouble,' a reference to the *Acts of the Apostles*: 'For before these days rose up Theudas, boasting himself to be somebody.' Churchill made it clear that the Queen could not sanction the marriage. So Townsend was sent away to Brussels, where he stayed for two years. By the time he returned in 1955, when the British public were agog to know whether the marriage would take place, the path of love had completely run its course. This is the main theme of episode 10.

Minor mistakes – The costume department gave Townsend his CVO, but failed to give the actor playing Lascelles any medals or Orders (by 1953 he was entitled to a GCVO, CMG, MC and various other medals); in Rhodesia, there was a Governor-type figure in a Guards tunic with a GCB, but only bar ribbons for medals. At one point we see the telephone switchboard, which includes Highgrove House. This is the house that the Duchy of Cornwall bought for Prince Charles in 1980, so it would not have been on the switchboard in the 1950s.

EPISODE 7

'Scientia Potentia Est'

It is 1940 and the Princesses are with their French governess. Princess Elizabeth goes to Eton College to be instructed by the Provost, Sir Henry Marten (not Vice-Provost as stated in the series). This leads to the Queen wishing to be better educated – knowledge is power – and as the story moves on into 1953, one of the themes is that she wants a tutor to help expand her general knowledge. Martin Charteris arranges such a figure called Professor Hodge, but he is a completely fictitious character. The Queen did not seek a tutor to help her, and nor would she ever have taken advice on constitutional matters from a figure outside the Palace system.

Retirement, or rather non-retirement, is in the air. Churchill is getting old and rather desperate, but refusing to go. The Anthony Eden character is ill in Boston – rather luridly so. He is taking injections, the implication being that he was almost a drug addict (a theme which gets worse in subsequent episodes). Then Churchill has two strokes. Evidently the Queen is not informed, and so the fictitious Hodge urges her to summon Churchill and Lord Salisbury to tick them off like recalcitrant schoolboys. *The Crown* plays out the two wiggings. Symbolically this is to demonstrate that the Queen is getting on top of her role as an assured constitutional monarch.

Tommy Lascelles is also about to retire. In this series, the Queen wants her former Private Secretary, Martin Charteris, to take over, and even offers him the job. He and his wife (Gay in real life, but here carelessly called Mary – the name of his daughter) go to look at the Private Secretary's new home at St James's Palace and have a tree trimmed outside it. They even say the house will be good for 'the girls'. (In real life they had the one daughter and two sons). Michael Adeane hears about this, is aggrieved, and complains to Lascelles, who engineers that Adeane succeeds him and not Charteris. Once again Lascelles proves himself more dominant and the Queen's private wishes are set aside.

This is inaccurate. It is traditional that the monarch's serving Private Secretary stays on for a few months at the beginning of a new reign to help with the transition, as did Lascelles until after the Coronation, retiring at the age of sixty-six on the last day of 1953. Michael Adeane and Martin Charteris were working as a team (along with Edward Ford, who is not portrayed in the series). Michael Adeane was always the natural successor, and there was no fuss. He took over.

In this episode, the film-makers have put a 1972 story into a 1953 context, presumably so that they could use the Lascelles figure. There was a fuss over Adeane's successor when he retired. At that time Charteris was the natural successor, but Lord Cobbold, a former Governor of the Bank of England, wanted to sweep away the Guards Officer Old Etonian types who held sway in the Palace, and replace them with more meritocratic types. He tried to reject Charteris in favour of Philip Moore. But Charteris went to see the Queen and asked to take over. She immediately agreed, and he proved to be an inspired Private Secretary, who succeeded perhaps better than any other Private Secretary in presenting her to the world as she really is. He served until 1977.

The message that emerges from this episode is that the Queen is conscientious, prepared to do her homework and research, with a knack for discovering the truth when it is kept from her – as, for example, with Churchill's two strokes (though Lord Salisbury is unlikely to have been wilfully withholding this information from her).

Lascelles is well played in the series, though his older daughter (now ninety-four) has said that his hair parting is wrong and his moustache too big. By curious misfortune, the actor playing Michael Adeane looks more like the real life Martin Charteris.

EPISODE 8

'Pride And Joy'

The King used to say of his two daughters: 'Lilibet is my pride, and Margaret my joy.' (This is something first published in my biography of the Queen Mother, and therefore explains the title of this episode.) Here there is a complete jumble of the real life facts. The episode starts with a scene where the Queen unveils a statue of King George VI in the Mall. This was in fact unveiled on 6 October 1955. But suddenly plans are being made for the Commonwealth tour of 1953 and 1954, so the story moves back in time.

There is particular discussion about Gibraltar as a place that could be dangerous. This was quite true. There were threats from the Spanish, and for a visit of less than two days, there were detectives from Scotland Yard operating under cover there for several months. There are some scenes from the Commonwealth tour demonstrating the Queen's determination to undertake it all, and the strain this put on her. At one point the press see the Queen and

84

Prince Philip emerging from a house after a row. Rightly, they stress the success of the tour.

The film-makers decided that while the Queen was away on her Commonwealth tour, the country would be run by Princess Margaret, rather than the Queen Mother. They use her as a modernizer, breaking all the rules and introducing a spontaneous and touchy-feely (quasi-Diana, Princess of Wales) approach to being Head of State which, not surprisingly, upsets everyone. She rewrites a speech, suiting her wayward personality and introducing more colour into it, and delivers this at an Ambassadors' reception (curiously, British Ambassadors serving overseas, in Washington and Athens, who appear to have flown in for this party). She gets the guests laughing. The point they seek to make is that Princess Margaret thinks she would make a better Queen than her sister, more in tune with the changing times. The Charteris figure gets more and more worried as she chats to miners, gives spontaneous interviews to the media in which she mentions her affection for Townsend, and takes a dig at the Queen. She gets ticked off by Churchill, who begins to detect a crisis arising, akin to the Abdication. When the Queen comes back, Churchill alerts her to Princess Margaret's behaviour.

None of the above happened and is ultimately tabloid invention. Nor do I subscribe to the idea that there was bitter jealousy between Princess Margaret and the Queen. Princess Margaret always supported her sister.

To achieve this, they blur the dates. They have the

Queen Mother out of the way, buying Barrogill Castle (later renamed the Castle of Mey) in Scotland, something which actually happened a whole year earlier, in 1952. Lascelles (who would by then have retired) tells the Queen Mother what her duties will be, but she tells him she wants to be away. The episode twists history by suggesting the Queen Mother was prepared to shirk all her responsibilities.

In reality the Queen Mother was very much in London while the Queen was away, not least looking after Prince Charles and Princess Anne, who stayed with her at Royal Lodge most weekends (when she was not away racing), and at Sandringham for a long Christmas holiday. She was the senior Counsellor of State during the Queen's absence. Counsellors act in tandem and Princess Margaret usually assisted her. Churchill had the same kind of audiences with the Queen Mother as he would have done with the Queen, but not so regularly. The series also has Princess Margaret being advised by Martin Charteris, when in real life, he was travelling with the Queen and Prince Philip.

As to the Castle of Mey scenes, the Queen Mother did not ride horses after the early 1930s, so to see her cantering along the beaches is somewhat strange. Nor is it likely that the castle's funny old owner, Captain Imbert-Terry, would not have recognised her. While she stays with the Vyners, she addresses the issues of her early widowhood. As this is meant to be late 1953, and not 1952, this does not convince – even with dramatic licence.

Minor mistakes – at a fitting they dress Prince Philip in the naval uniform which he wore but once – at the Coronation – an outdated uniform with epaulettes; later, he wears a Garter riband and bar medals, which is incorrect. The Caribbean Governor in white is wearing what might be a curious interpretation of a military GBE riband along with a huge GCMG star. When Princess Margaret gives her speech, the guests are wearing Orders, but she is not.

EPISODE 9

'Assassins'

In London in 1954, Jean Wallop, a private person alive when this episode was first shown – (she died on 11 April 2019) – arrives in a restaurant to dine with Lord Porchester (later 7th Earl of Carnarvon). He proposes to her. She accepts on one condition – that he does not still hold a torch for 'her' – i.e. the Queen. I have it on impeccable authority that the future Lady Carnarvon did not even realise that he knew the Queen when she met him. The outcome of this scene is that he tells her that for the Queen there was only ever Prince Philip, and she (his bride to be) is the only one for him. The Porchesters were married in January 1956.

The Crown suggests that Porchester was the man many wanted the Queen to marry, and they hint that she would have been happier with him than with Prince Philip. For the record, the Queen Mother originally wanted Princess Elizabeth to marry a Grenadier Guards officer. The late

Duke of Grafton springs to mind. But from very early on, she set her heart on the good-looking Prince Philip. In 1947 they were engaged. The Queen Mother told Sir Arthur Penn, 'Won't the Grenadier Guards be disappointed?' They were, and at first refused to have Prince Philip as their Colonel.

The episode depicts Porchester ringing the Queen late at night, with a certain number of double entendres, his wife-to-be coming through from the bathroom. The Queen's love of racing is emphasized, as is Prince Philip's boredom with it. This theme is rather dropped as the episode goes on, though in one scene, the Queen and Prince Philip watch a mare being covered, with Lord Porchester observing from afar and giving some predictably cheap lines. Afterwards Prince Philip jumps out of the Land Rover in a rage. This is followed by a scene back home, with a declaration of love by the Queen for Prince Philip.

Lord Carnarvon was a close adviser to the Queen, as her racing manager, and she often stayed with him and his wife to visit studs in the Berkshire area. Both she and Prince Philip flew down from Balmoral to attend his funeral in 2001.

The Graham Sutherland story is well told. Sutherland was commissioned to paint Churchill's portrait, to be presented to him in Westminster Hall for his eightieth birthday on 30 November 1954. Peter Morgan is on firm ground here, as it is within the political domain. Intermingled with this is the theme that Churchill should stand down. There is a fictional scene where Eden visits Churchill at Chartwell, and bids him to give way in a histrionic, hysterical manner – presaging the recurring theme that he was some kind of junkie. As to the portrait itself, it was revealed after her death in 1977 that Lady Churchill had destroyed it. In 1957 she described Churchill's reaction to the painting in a letter to Lord Beaverbrook: 'It wounded him deeply that this brilliant…painter with whom he had made friends while sitting for him should see him as a gross & cruel monster.'

There is a partly fictitious version of the speech he gave in Westminster Hall, in which he teases the audience that he is about to retire and that his successor, Anthony Eden, is to hand. It appears that he then promptly resigns, and with the brutality of the political system, as he leaves the Palace, Eden's car draws up. The Queen's speech at Churchill's farewell dinner was taken from a private letter from the Queen to Churchill after his resignation and not delivered as such on the night. As we listen to it, we see another scene: Lady Churchill presiding over the burning of the Sutherland portrait.

In reality Churchill did not resign immediately after his birthday in November 1954. He hung on in office until April 1955.

EPISODE 10

'Gloriana'

The episode reprises the events of December 1936. Edward VIII agrees to see his brother, the Duke of York, but not the Duchess (there is no evidence for that). Then the new King informs his daughters that their uncle has put love before duty. He tells them never to let each other down, thus introducing the theme that there could be tension between them later on.

A Royal Standard is hoisted over Balmoral. It is Princess Margaret's twenty-fifth birthday (21 August 1955), and she declares she still feels the same way about Group Captain Townsend. It seems possible that she can now marry him. But the Queen discusses the Royal Marriages Act with Michael Adeane. He invokes a different version of the situation. He mentions that both Houses of Parliament need to be informed and that if they object, she would need to wait for twelve months. Still under the illusion that she is free to marry, Princess Margaret wants to announce it.

Another scene shows Prince Philip teaching Prince Charles to fish, so that we realise that he is quite tough on the boy. The Queen Mother voices the opinion that Prince Philip is taking it out on Charles due to the frustrations of his own life. *The Crown* likes to think that the Queen Mother was very thick with Lascelles in his retirement. She relied on him a bit after the King's death but Lascelles took a dim view of her philosophy of life, considering it was best summed up in the hymn: 'the rich man in his castle, the poor man at his gate.' But it gives them the idea that Prince Philip was sent by the Queen to open the Olympic Games in Melbourne, Australia in November 1956 to get him out of the way: away from bullying his son and in the hope, as expressed clearly in this episode, that he would come back 'changed'. But this all happens in August 1955 and he did not undertake the voyage until October 1956.

The second and final round in the Princess Margaret/ Peter Townsend drama is played out. We see headlines speculating as to whether or not she is going to marry the Group Captain. Apparently Prince Philip is somewhat in league with Princess Margaret over the marriage question. Townsend returns and they run together in a passionate embrace. Then come the problems, the involvement of the Attorney-General, the threat that Lord Salisbury will resign if the marriage takes place, the Queen saying she will support her in any way she can, but then that she would be deprived of money and titles, and have to live abroad for several years as Mrs Peter Townsend. Princess

Margaret claims the country is on her side. The invented words of their father about mutual support are repeated by the Queen.

Then it all gets worse, with the Cabinet advising against the marriage, the Archbishop of Canterbury and other Bishops reminding the Queen that she is Defender of the Faith and of the oath made at the Coronation, and finally the Queen seeking advice from the Duke of Windsor in France. He tells her 'You must protect the kingdom'. And so, in this episode, the Queen's line is that Princess Margaret cannot marry Townsend and remain part of the family.

In reality, Eden did advise the Queen at Balmoral, but there was no involvement from the Archbishop, and the Duke of Windsor was in no position to pontificate about the roles of sister or Queen, or of duty to the realm.

The film-makers maintain that Princess Margaret broke off from Townsend because she had been forbidden to marry him. Furthermore, she tells him she will never marry anyone else. And then Townsend makes a public statement, in fact reading much of the written statement that in reality Princess Margaret issued to the press. He then returns to Brussels.

In truth, the decision was a mutual one between Princess Margaret and the Group Captain, largely based on the fact that Lascelles's separation plan had worked and the love between them had died.

None of the characters are happy at the end of this

episode. Princess Margaret is seen depressed at parties, and Peter Townsend sitting forlornly alone in his apartment in Brussels. Prince Philip is angry at being sent away on the long tour.

The situation with Nasser in Egypt is flagged up during this episode. We see meetings with Eden, more pills being taken, and in the end, Anthony Eden slumped in front of burning cine-film of Nasser, having just stuck a needle full of drugs into his arm. This is followed by an image of the Queen posing in tiara and evening dress next to the Crown Jewels, which have been brought to the Palace for effect. She is shown as an assured and confident young monarch, while the ever-frustrated Prince Philip drives off down the Mall in his open car, all alone, looking distinctly fed up.

I should be grateful that it is Cecil Beaton who gets the last word in both this series and Series 2, extolling the virtues of monarchy with Shakespearian lines. Nevertheless, Claire Foy's Queen looks ominously sad.

Viewers then had to wait a year to find out why.

SEASON 2

The next ten episodes of *The Crown* were released on 8 December 2017.

EPISODE I

'Misadventure'

Series 2 opens with a scene implying that the marriage of the Queen and Prince Philip was so desperate that they would have liked to divorce. There is much talk of Prince Philip playing second fiddle, complaining, whingeing, and whining, and the Queen feeling humiliated. This scene comes after the voyage in *Britannia* in October 1956, when he went to open the Olympic Games in Melbourne and then toured the South Atlantic. It then flashes back to scenes before the trip, and includes a contrived moment when the Queen puts a cine camera into his briefcase and discovers a photograph of a ballerina. Pre-publicity for *The Crown* suggested that this ballerina was a creation of fiction, but, most improbably, the series named her as Galina Ulanova, the feisty *prima ballerina assoluta* of the Bolshoi Ballet, very much a real person.

Young television viewers will not have heard of Ulanova, but she was immensely famous. Her 1956 visit with the

Bolshoi was the cultural event of the season, almost as exciting at the time as Nureyev's arrival in 1962. David Webster, Director of Covent Garden, described her and her visit as 'a miracle.' The Bolshoi came to London after nine years of negotiations, and Margot Fonteyn and the Sadler's Wells Ballet went to dance in Moscow. She was more proficient and distinguished than beautiful. The ballet dancer Antoinette Sibley described her: 'She was a mess. She looked like an old lady...this old woman got up from the stalls. We thought she was the ballet mistress.' Born in 1910, Ulanova was then 46 years old, and it is impossible that Prince Philip could have met her, as she had never been to England before. Her only contact with Britain was an English teddy bear her mother had bought her when she was two. Ulanova arrived in Britain on 1 October, and Prince Philip came down from Sandringham on 9 October and left for his trip on 15 October. Ulanova was accompanied on this trip at all times by her husband.

The Queen Mother took Prince Charles to a matinée. Princess Margaret went and so did the Edens. The Queen attended alone on 25 October, when Ulanova chose to dance *Gisèle* for her, as it was the role in which she was most proficient.

Later in the episode Princess Margaret refers disparagingly to the Thursday Club, and goes so far as to suggest that an osteopath (clearly Dr Stephen Ward – see episode 10) procured ballerinas and others for the members. Ulanova was one of the ballet's most successful stars, and the suggestion (vague as it is) that such a distinguished, not to say matronly, ballet dancer might have been a Stephen Ward protégée is completely wide of the mark.

The other theme of the episode is the Suez crisis: Anthony Eden, his potentially duplicitous role in the crisis, Nasser, the Israeli involvement, Mountbatten advising the Queen, Anthony Nutting giving words of warning, and secret deals with the French. Here Peter Morgan is on stronger ground, as he has Robert Lacey as his historical adviser, and Lacey spoke to Lord Mountbatten when researching his book, *Majesty* (1977). In the Hartley Library in Southampton is a letter from Lacey to Mountbatten, assuring him that there is no danger of him being identified as the source about Eden and Suez for his book. What Mountbatten told him was that the Queen disapproved of Eden's policy, and when Eden (by then Lord Avon) read this in serialisation he threatened to sue Lacey. Martin Charteris stepped in to soothe ruffled feathers. Maybe the Queen did know, but Mountbatten did not always tell the truth, particularly to authors.

Then the episode portrays Princess Margaret, still drunk the morning after another late night partying, and still blaming the Queen for her unhappiness on account of the Peter Townsend debacle from Series 1. There are gratuitous reminders of the infidelity of Edwina Mountbatten with Nehru. And the theme is introduced that Eileen Parker is unhappy about the prolonged absence from family life of her husband, Mike Parker, who is travelling with Prince Philip. That was indeed the case.

EPISODE 2

'A Company of Men'

This episode concentrates on Prince Philip's voyage in *Britannia* between October 1956 and February 1957, more or less ignoring the official stopovers and making it appear that he hated formality and was only happy playing games such as cricket and tug-of-war. There are scenes with him dancing and watching bare-breasted girls dancing. There is a grainy image of a man descending onto one of these women for sex – hard to see, but probably the Mike Parker character. There is a scene in which a Tongan man is rescued, and Prince Philip has *Britannia* turned round to take him home: a chance for more bright-eyed local girls to lure him to dance. There is no evidence for this. A journalist called Helen King is invented to interview the Prince in Australia, and he clearly accepts the invitation to talk to her in order to seduce her. She annoys him with her questions and he storms out, but the implication is clear. At one point the trip is summed up as 'a five-month stag night – whores in every port.'

An incriminating message is read out by Baron to the Thursday Club amidst raucous laughter. We see Eileen Parker getting hold of a girl who works at the club, and asking for evidence against her husband, Mike. The girl hands over the letter. The Queen is even seen calling unexpectedly on Mrs Parker at her home, only to be told in no uncertain terms that she, Mrs Parker, has sacrificed enough for the Royal Family. She goes to her lawyer and starts the process of separation leading to divorce. There was no visit by the Queen to Mrs Parker.

In 1982 Eileen Parker wrote a book called *Step Aside for Royalty*, a frank account of her experiences, aiming to set the record straight. This makes it clear that her main resentment was that her husband was away too much with Prince Philip, missing family anniversaries, and generally finding his life as a Private Secretary more interesting than being with her. She hints at Parker's infidelity, but she certainly did not obtain any evidence of this in 1956. Furthermore, there can have been no letter for Baron to read out to the raucous company of the Thursday Club, not least because Baron (Stirling Henry Nahum) had died on 5 September 1956, and Prince Philip and Mike Parker did not set off for their trip until 15 October.

In his posthumously published memoirs, Baron took credit for founding the Thursday Club after the war. He wrote: 'I suggested forming a little club to lighten the gloom that surrounded us all, and that we should meet with friends once a week. No issues of importance would be allowed, no international questions would be solved. The club would be devoted to absolute Inconsequence. We would eat as well as we could, tell stories and swop reminiscences…The lunches lasted well into the afternoon, spreading consternation and dismay through our liver-systems and playing havoc with afternoon appointments.' Mrs Parker described it as 'a luncheon club organised by Prince Philip and Mike for entertaining kindred spirits'. She continued: 'They would meet for long meandering lunches at Wheeler's in Soho and entertain themselves during the meal with speeches, pranks and jokes.' Mrs Parker wrote that the Queen referred to the members as 'Philip's funny friends.' That is all she wrote about the Thursday Club.

This episode also contains two Christmas speeches, one by Prince Philip from *Britannia* and one from the Queen at Sandringham. These cryptic messages are exchanged over the air waves, the Prince Philip character saying: 'We are men together, but we each stand alone.' Arguably the speeches devised for *The Crown* were warmer and more human, even better, in fact, than those actually delivered. The real life Prince Philip said: 'We are absent, most of us, because there is a Commonwealth…I hope all of you at Sandringham are enjoying a very happy Christmas and I hope you children are having a lot of fun. I am sorry I am not with you.' He ended on a religious theme: 'We pray, in words used thousands of years ago, that the Lord watch between me and thee when we are absent from each other.'

The real Queen sent a greeting to him and all serving on

Britannia: 'If my husband cannot be at home on Christmas Day, I could not wish for a better reason than that he should be travelling in other parts of the Commonwealth… On his voyage back to England, he will call at some of the least accessible parts of the world, those islands of the South Atlantic separated from us by immense stretches of the ocean, yet linked to us with bonds of brotherhood and trust.'

The rest of this episode is involved with the Suez crisis, with Eden relying more heavily on pentobarbitane pills. There are suggestions that the Queen's two private secretaries, Michael Adeane and Martin Charteris, acted as spies on the Queen's behalf.

Minor mistake – as an Admiral of the Fleet Prince Philip would be entitled to fly the Union Flag, rather than a White Ensign, on *Britannia*.

EPISODE 3

'Lisbon'

The first issue is the return of the Prime Minister, Anthony Eden, from a recuperative break in Jamaica. He thinks he can resume office, but Harold Macmillan turns on him. 'There's no justice in politics,' Macmillan tells him. Eden realises the game is up and resigns. The Queen reiterates an earlier theme, by suggesting that Eden wanted to make a name for himself by going to war in Suez – emerging, as it were, from Churchill's shadow. She also makes it clear to Macmillan, when he becomes Prime Minister, that she is aware that previously he had supported the war. Despite a bit of dramatic license here, it is generally accepted that Macmillan turned on Eden, and certainly Eden's wife never forgave him.

There is more espionage in the Private Secretary's office, Tommy Lascelles being brought into play to manage the Parker crisis. In this episode, it is suggested that Mrs Parker is suing for divorce, at which point, on board *Britannia*, an angry Prince Philip informs Mike Parker: 'You know the rules,' and demands his instant resignation. Parker leaves *Britannia* in Gibraltar.

In reality Eileen Parker sought a separation, rather than a divorce. According to her book, she did not intend this to become public knowledge while her husband was at sea with Prince Philip, but her lawyer, Meryn Lewis, put out a statement without consulting her – he gave a scoop to Rex North of the *Sunday Pictorial*. As a result, Parker's marriage came to an end and so did his career as a royal courtier, something which Mrs Parker maintained she had not intended to happen. In her book, Eileen Parker wrote: 'I learned that both Prince Philip and the Queen had tried to dissuade Mike from resigning.' But his solicitor stated: 'With all the worry in the present circumstances of his marriage he feels he cannot give of his best.'

His courtier life did not end immediately. He stayed on with Prince Philip for some months, was invested with a CVO by the Queen in March, and was in attendance when Prince Philip attended the wedding of his niece, Princess Margarita, in Baden in June 1957. When Mrs Parker finally sued for divorce in 1958, she cited a certain Mrs Thompson for adultery (in July 1957). Following the divorce, Eileen immediately married a man called Tom Prentice, who worked for Stanley Rous at the Football Association, which may partly explain her wish to move on. Parker himself did not remarry until 1962.

There is no evidence of Lascelles being involved in any

of this. But in real life an announcement was given to the press a week after Parker's resignation on 5 February – therefore on 12 February: 'It is quite untrue that there is any rift between the Queen and the Duke.'

Their marriage has now lasted over seventy years.

Towards the end of the episode, the imagined show-down between the Queen and Prince Philip is repeated. It ends with him demanding to be given new status. And there is a Camelot-style scene where he is invested with a sword of state, a ring, and a sceptre, crowned with a ducal coronet (such as he had worn at the Coronation four years earlier), with what looks suspiciously like a Baron's robes draped over him. As we know, he was already a Duke.

Prince Philip has never been interested in titles, least of all for himself. The main reason to create him a Prince of the United Kingdom was that George VI had forgot-ten to do so, when he created him HRH and Duke of Edinburgh in 1947. Lord Mountbatten wanted it and so did Prince Philip's aunt, Queen Louise of Sweden, who was disappointed that he had turned it down in 1955. Mountbatten wrote to her in 1957: 'Lilibet has got the new Prime Minister – in consultation with Commonwealth colleagues – to ask for Philip to be made "The Prince" on return from this tour, & we all hope he'll agree this time.' The honour was given to recognise his service to the Commonwealth on the long voyage. To portray him as demanding the status is wrong.

The Crown's conclusion is that the marriage continued

in quest of the survival of the monarchy. Peter Morgan considers that one of their principal interests is their own survival. There is an alternative view – that they devote their lives to the service of the nation and Commonwealth. The Queen has also played a significant role as a conciliator internationally, particularly with countries such as Germany, Japan, Russia and China, and, more recently in the public memory, with Ireland.

Minor mistakes – Sir Michael Adeane retained his moustache in real life; Cecil Beaton never photographed Prince Philip (other than at the Coronation); the *Britannia* trip lasted four months, not five.

EPISODE 4

'Beryl'

Colin Tennant weds Lady Anne Coke at St Withburga's, Holkham, on 21 April 1956. Princess Margaret is there with the Queen Mother (they both were), and present with his camera is the young Antony Armstrong-Jones. By now miserable after having lost Townsend, she agrees half-heartedly to marry Billy Wallace, a member of the Margaret set. This goes wrong later when Wallace (depicted as a coward) fights a duel with Colin Tennant and is wounded. There was no such duel in real life. But in the episode, Princess Margaret ditches Wallace, and afterwards we see her staggering around in her bedroom, whisky in hand, looking completely demented.

Later, Cecil Beaton (poorly dressed compared to the real Cecil) comes to photograph her, and is given some prosaic lines about his approach to the fantasy of beauty as he poses her. The results are stunning but she does not like them. Enter Lady Elizabeth Cavendish, her 'new'

Lady-in-Waiting (in fact appointed in October 1954), who invites her to a dinner where she meets Tony again. He flirts with her and invites her to be photographed. There follow meandering scenes in his studio, where he subtly disconcerts her and makes her fall in love with him. Another bedroom scene shows her back home, much happier, clearly in love. Tony takes her photo, with naked shoulders – the one shown was actually taken ten years later in 1967, after their marriage in 1960. They ride about on motorbikes, and yes, they did do that.

It is true that Lady Elizabeth Cavendish introduced Princess Margaret to her more Bohemian friends in the hope of amusing her. She produced Tony Armstrong-Jones, but she, like many others, was greatly surprised when they married, as that had not been part of the plan.

There is a further scene in which the new Prime Minister, Harold Macmillan, talks of the importance of good relations with the Americans, telling the Queen of the importance of sustaining a good 'marriage' in international politics. This gives the film-makers the chance to point out the problems in his own marriage. His wife, Lady Dorothy, has been pursuing a long affair with the politician, Bob Boothby, and they drop in the canard that her daughter Sarah (later Heath, who died in 1970) might have been Boothby's love-child.

Macmillan was tortured for forty-five years by the suspicion that Sarah was Boothby's child. When Sarah was born in 1930, Dorothy told him that Boothby was the father in order to get him to leave her. This would have ruined his political career. The marriage survived. In 1975, nine years after Dorothy's death in 1966, and five years after Sarah's tragic death following a fall, Macmillan ran into Boothby at Julian Amery's house in Eaton Square. He asked for a private meeting with Boothby, who assured him that Sarah was a Macmillan. As D.R. Thorpe put it in his biography *Supermac*: 'Boothby was a rakish figure, but in one thing he was very careful. Despite – or perhaps because of – having so many affairs, he ensured he never left behind what the Victorians would have called "a vestige".'

EPISODE 5

'Marionettes'

This episode ends with a real life photograph of John Grigg, the former Lord Altrincham, and professes that Buckingham Palace maintained that he had done more to help the monarchy than any other figure in the twentieth century. In this episode we have an accurate portrayal of Altrincham's attack on the Queen, how he was slapped across the face by a member of the League of Empire Loyalists, and how his words caused a major re-think within the Palace walls.

The true course of events was that Malcolm Muggeridge had written about 'The Royal Soap Opera' in *The New Statesman* in October 1955. This caused minimal stir, but Altrincham's article in *The National and Evening Review* in August 1957 turned him into an arch-villain overnight, causing Muggeridge's piece to be reprinted with a similar effect. Altrincham received 2,000 letters of complaint, was anathematized by the Archbishop of Canterbury, menaced with many threats and, yes, he was slapped by an elderly member of the League of Empire Loyalists.

Altrincham was far from anti-monarchist, but he saw the need for change. He attacked the Queen's education and the monarchy's way of life: 'the London season, racing, the grouse moor, Canasta and the occasional royal tour.' He lambasted presentation parties at which debutantes paraded in front of the Queen as a 'grotesque survival from the past'. He saw the monarchy as being able to fire the popular imagination, 'not just as a symbol of stability and continuity, but as a positive force for good in the world.' This led directly to a number of changes – the abolition of presentation parties, appointments to the Royal Household from different walks of life, the informal luncheon parties, and so on.

This episode introduces the fantasy that the Queen made a dire speech at a Jaguar factory, written by Michael Adeane with the approval of Lascelles. The Queen and Duke did visit the Jaguar factory near Coventry on the same day that she laid the foundation stone for the new cathedral – 23 March 1956. But there is no evidence of a speech, nor is there evidence of the Queen engineering a face-to-face meeting with Altrincham to discuss his article. Nor would the first guests coming to an informal luncheon have come along in morning coats and garden party hats.

EPISODE 6

'Vergangenheit'

Vergangenheit means 'the past', so episode 6 kicks off with dramatic scenes (and thriller music, as for a John Le Carré adaptation) as a captured German officer shows where he buried a vital tin box containing the Marburg Papers, which were deemed to contain material proving that the Duke of Windsor had been a traitor to his country during the Second World War.

The episode introduces the Queen's interest in the evangelist, the Rev Billy Graham. He represents the spirit of forgiveness, which is concerning the Queen in respect of the Duke of Windsor. She invites Graham to preach and afterwards they talk. As the episode progresses, the Queen asks him about forgiveness, since she has been considering forgiving her uncle.

The episode employs a device to create conflict. It tells a version of the Marburg Papers saga. It then depicts the Duke of Windsor asking the Queen to sanction him to get a job. As would be expected, every possible accusation is aired against the Duke – particularly in a scene when the Queen asks Tommy Lascelles to spill it all out, which he does: Mrs Simpson having an affair with Ribbentrop, Hess wanting to reinstate the Duke as King, the Duke visiting concentration camps on his 1937 visit to Germany, holding the Duke personally responsible for the German occupation of Paris, and so on. At the end of the programme, to back up their point, they show some real photos of the Duke on his German visit, to convince the viewer that all this happened.

So where is the truth in any of this? The Marburg Papers did exist and extracts were published from time to time, causing the Duke of Windsor considerable annoyance in the 1950s and 1960s. When the first batch was published by the Americans in 1954, Churchill told the Duke that they were harmless and had been put in 'to add some sensationalism to what would otherwise be a very boring book.' More came out later, but to little avail. As Philip Ziegler, the Duke's official biographer, put it: 'Many other fantasies have been voiced in the last thirty years. The laws of libel mercifully ensured that the most grotesque have only been published after his [the Duke's] death.'

Then there is the question of the Duke's quest for a job. On his return from the Bahamas in 1945 the Duke did try to get a job, and he also repeated his request that the Duchess be made an HRH and received by the King and Queen. He was put firmly in his place by Tommy Lascelles, who asked him not to continually plead for these things. The Duke wriggled a bit, but in effect he did go away. Presently he settled at the house in the Bois (here called the Villa Windsor, a name it was only given years later by Fayed), and also bought his Mill outside Paris. There were never any plots to make him Ambassador in Paris, or a roving Commissioner for the Commonwealth.

This episode has a fantasy that the Duke was not allowed to come to Britain without the Sovereign's permission. This is untrue, and he came whenever he pleased, but obviously informally. The Windsors stayed with the Earl of Dudley, they went to see *Oliver* on stage, etc., and in 1965 he spent some time in the London Clinic for an eye operation, when the Queen visited him twice. In June 1967 the Duke got his longed-for meeting with the Royal Family, when both appeared for the unveiling of the memorial to Queen Mary in the wall of Marlborough House. By an agreement made in 1961, the Queen permitted them both to be buried at Frogmore. He died in 1972 and she in 1986.

There was no question of the Queen sending him away as a traitor, as she does towards the end of this episode. The vilification of the Duke is completed with the Prince Philip character congratulating the Queen for 'banishing Satan from entering the Garden of Eden.' The Duke may have been out of his depth, but he was no traitor.

EPISODE 7

'Matrimonium'

The scene is Brussels in August 1959, and Group Captain Peter Townsend is preparing to marry a nineteen-year-old girl called Marie-Luce Jamagne. This episode concerns the somewhat unconventional courtship of Princess Margaret and Tony Armstrong-Jones, and is full of quasi-erotic scenes – Tony with Jacqui Chan, Tony with Princess Margaret, and Tony lying on a bed with Camilla Fry, along with his first choice of best man, her husband, Jeremy Fry. Obviously there is a lot of dramatic licence here, since no-one knows what goes on behind closed doors in bedrooms (or in photographic studios, for that matter). We are treated to a bare-breasted Camilla Fry, the buttocks of her husband, Jeremy, as he joins her and a naked Tony on the bed, and a fair amount of sexual activity in the studio, not only with Jacqui Chan but also with Princess Margaret. One scene with Jacqui Chan is heralded with Tony sporting an erection concealed within his white trousers.

It is hard to keep up with Tony Armstrong-Jones's amatory exploits, but we now know a lot more following Anne de Courcy's 2008 biography of him. In the series, the Queen gives a lavish party and gets suspicious about Mrs Fry. She asks Michael Adeane to investigate, and he turns to Tommy Lascelles to help form the case against Armstrong-Jones. They inform the Queen about Jacqui Chan, Robin Banks, Gina Ward, and both Mr and Mrs Jeremy Fry.

In real life Tony had had an affair with the actress Jacqui Chan, but that was over by 1960. She was invited to his wedding. Robin Banks was a one-time long-suffering assistant. She did not have an affair with him, as she was in love with someone else. Georgina Ward, a lovely actress, did have an affair with him, but most complicated of all was his relationship with the Frys.

It was revealed many years later that Tony was the father of Camilla Fry's daughter, Polly, who was born on 28 May 1960, three weeks after his wedding. For the record, Jeremy Fry was asked to step down as Tony's best man. His place was taken by Dr Roger Gilliat. This was due to a homosexual conviction – 'importuning for immoral purposes'. Fry was from the Quaker chocolate family. In 1955 he had married Camilla Grinling. They had two sons and two daughters before divorcing in 1967. Camilla died in 2000, and Jeremy in 2005.

It demonstrates a certain amount of chutzpah on the part of Armstrong-Jones that he went to the altar of Westminster Abbey to marry the Queen's sister when, if he gave it a thought, he might have realised that he had just begat a child on his best friend's wife. Fortunately, Princess Margaret never knew about the paternity of Mrs Fry's daughter.

There are two points which make something of a nonsense of this episode. The first is the conceit that Tony only married Princess Margaret to gain the approval of his mother, Anne, Countess of Rosse. It is evidently true that Tony thought his mother did not respect him. Her character is played by a good actress, Anna Chancellor, except that in real life Lady Rosse was much too practised a performer on the social scene ever to portray what she was really thinking. She lived in a dream-like world of her own imagination, lying in bed in the mornings writing long handwritten letters to friends, and conjuring descriptions of her brother, Oliver Messel, as 'Darling Angel Oliver'. In real life she was somewhat more than pleased about the marriage to Princess Margaret. She herself had risen from being Anne Messel to Countess of Rosse, and society called her 'Tugboat Annie' on the grounds that she 'drifted from peer to peer.'

Another conceit is that Princess Margaret was determined to marry before Townsend. He got engaged in October 1959 and married Marie-Luce on 21 December. Princess Margaret did not get engaged until February 1960, and the film-makers have invented some dodgy protocol that the engagement could not be made public until Prince Andrew was born, since they decide that no announcement can be made 'until the Sovereign's child is born.' It is true, however, that the Queen asked for the announcement to come after Prince Andrew's birth. But it seems that Tony and Princess Margaret agreed to marry somewhat after Townsend's announcement of his engagement.

EPISODE 8

'Dear Mrs Kennedy'

Here is a chance to see the workings of the Commonwealth. The episode opens with President Nkrumah in full voice in Accra, declaring that Ghana is a free country, and that they are all Africans. The Queen's picture is taken down, and one of Lenin is put up in its place. Part of the issue is where Ghana will side – with the Russians or with the Americans, and whether it will stay in the Commonwealth.

Two other themes are brought into play here. One is the Queen observing an old oak on the Balmoral estate, that has passed its best and must be felled – a filmic symbol of the decline of British influence in Africa. Then there is the visit of President John F. Kennedy and his wife, Jackie, to Paris. The Queen feels middle-aged, and the film-makers suggest that she felt insecure about Jackie Kennedy, jealous of her and threatened by her.

In the episode, the Kennedys are coming over to Britain, and the Queen and Prince Philip invite them to dine at

Buckingham Palace. Many of the male guests want to sit next to Jackie, but Prince Philip insists he should (which is of course correct etiquette). According to the episode, he flirts with Jackie. The Queen shows her round the Palace and is rather taken by her, but then discovers that Mrs Kennedy has made disparaging remarks, and presently the Queen prises these out of her friend and equerry, Lord Plunket. He tells her that Mrs Kennedy thought the Palace run-down, the institution of monarchy out-dated, and the Queen herself middle-aged, incurious, unintelligent and unremarkable.

It is apparently this that inspires the Queen to go out to Ghana and win Nkrumah round by dancing the foxtrot with him. She returns in triumph. The film-makers hit the message on the head by having JFK congratulate his wife on influencing the course of foreign policy – in that without the jibes the Queen would not have gone – and then there is an invented scene in which Mrs Kennedy comes to Windsor Castle to apologise and explain her ill-advised comments.

We then fast forward to see the oak being felled in the park. It is now November 1963 and the Queen and Prince Philip witness the events surrounding President Kennedy's assassination. The Queen breaks protocol by asking that the tenor bell at Westminster Abbey be sounded, something which only happens on the death of a member of the Royal Family or a Dean of Westminster. (The bell was duly sounded for an hour on Saturday 23 November).

Now we must examine the facts, since what they have

done in this episode is to take two independent events, both of which did happen (the dinner for the Kennedys on 5 June 1961 and the visit to Ghana between 9 and 20 November 1961), and clash them together to create a drama, throwing in the old oak tree for symbolic reasons.

The Queen entertained the Kennedys to dinner on 5 June. The President and his wife were coming to Britain for a private family christening for Jackie's niece, Christina Radziwill. Though it was not required that the Queen should entertain them, she offered to do so. There was a dinner party at Buckingham Palace and some question as to whether Stas and Lee Radziwill (Lee being Jackie's sister) should be invited, since both had been divorced. In the end the rule against inviting divorced people was relaxed, though a few days later the Queen's aunt, the Duchess of Gloucester, complained to her sister-in-law, the Duchess of Buccleuch, that the Queen had been forced to entertain 'some people called Radziwill' as if things were getting seriously out of hand.

There exist two sources for Jackie's disparaging comments. One is Gore Vidal's 1995 memoir, *Palimpsest*, in which he dug into some notes made in 1961 and added some afterthoughts. From other things written by Vidal, I suspect he may have subscribed to the Noël Coward philosophy of never letting the truth get in the way of a good story, but let's take him at face value. Evidently Jackie Kennedy told Vidal that the Queen had refused to invite either Princess Margaret or Princess Marina (both of whom the Kennedys wanted to see), but had produced a number of Commonwealth agriculture ministers. She found the Queen 'pretty heavy-going'. Gore Vidal added that he had repeated this to Princess Margaret years later, who said: 'But that's what she's there for.'

Here is Vidal's paragraph in full, the italics representing what he wrote in 1961:

'I think the queen resented me. Philip was nice, but nervous. One felt absolutely no relationship between them. The queen was human only once.' Jackie had been telling me about the Kennedy state visit to Canada and the rigors of being on view at all hours. ('I greeted Jack every day with a tear-stained face.') The queen looked rather conspiratorial and said, 'One gets crafty after a while and learns how to save oneself.' Then she said, 'You like pictures.' And she marched Jackie down a long gallery, stopping at a Van Dyk to say, 'That's a good horse.'

So, no flirting.

The night afterwards Jackie told Cecil Beaton, 'They were all tremendously kind and nice, but she was not impressed by the flowers, or the furnishings of the apartments at Buckingham Palace, or by the Queen's dark-blue tulle dress and shoulder straps, or her flat hair.'

The idea that Mrs Kennedy returned for a further meeting in order to explain herself to the Queen, as in the episode, is fabrication.

The Queen's proposed visit to Ghana was certainly a complicated issue. Nkrumah had been Prime Minister since 1952 and President since Ghana became a Republic in March 1957. He was becoming increasingly despotic. There were distinct fears that Ghana might leave the Commonwealth, as South Africa had done, as recently as 31 May 1961. There was a suggestion that the Russians might finance the Volta Dam project.

The Queen had been meant to go to Ghana earlier, but became pregnant with Prince Andrew, so had to cancel. She did not want to disappoint Nkrumah. Meanwhile he had visited Russia in October, the political climate was turbulent, two bombs had gone off in Accra, and there were genuine fears for the Queen's safety. Duncan Sandys, then Secretary of State for Commonwealth Relations, was sent out to test the water. All went well, and the Queen remained determined to go. Macmillan wrote of her: 'She loves her duty and means to be a Queen and not a puppet.' She told him, 'How silly I should look if I was scared to visit Ghana and then Khruschev went and had a good reception.' So she went, and as shown in the episode, melted Nkrumah by dancing with him at the state ball. After the visit Macmillan was able to telephone President Kennedy and tell him: 'I risked my Queen. You must risk your money.' As a result, the Americans financed the building of the Volta Dam, and Ghana stayed in the Commonwealth. This had nothing to do with upstaging Mrs Kennedy.

EPISODE 9

'Paterfamilias'

This centres around Prince Charles at Gordonstoun, so there are lots of muddy boots, bullying, freezing, wet dormitories, cold showers and exacting cross country runs. We know that Prince Charles hated his time at Gordonstoun, and most people conclude he would have been happier at Eton, where, in the fullness of time, he sent his own sons. So that is the first theme exploited with full (and acceptable) dramatic licence. Amusingly, however, Kurt Hahn, Prince Philip's headmaster, is still running Gordonstoun in 1961 – he would have been seventy-five years old by then. In reality he retired in 1953.

The clashing theme is Prince Philip at Gordonstoun. He was sent there in the 1930s after prep school at Cheam and a brief spell at school at Salem. Kurt Hahn moved to Gordonstoun to avoid Nazi Germany, and Prince Philip joined him there. Being a more robust figure than his eldest son, he thrived at the school, acquitted himself well, and there is an argument that it made him the self-reliant man he is today.

This episode introduces a further drama, which perverts the facts. We see the young Prince Philip flying in a plane with his sister, Princess Cécile of Hesse, and we are told she is a nervous flyer. Then Prince Philip gets into a scrape at school, punches a boy, and as a result of this, Cécile is again forced to fly to England (the implication being that, but for this apocryphal incident, she would not have flown) while heavily pregnant. The plane crashes and she is killed. Prince Philip attends the funeral – much is made of the Nazi atmosphere in Darmstadt (true), though he himself is a contrasting figure to the uniformed Nazis, in his black overcoat. At the reception afterwards, his be-monocled father, Prince Andrew of Greece, shouts at him, 'It's true, isn't it, boy? You're the reason we're all here burying my favourite child.'

The facts are as follows. Cécile and her family did fly to Britain, and they were all killed when the plane hit a factory chimney in fog near Ostend on 16 November 1937. But the reason they came was a long-planned commitment to attend the wedding of Cécile's brother-in-law, Prince Ludwig of Hesse, to Hon Margaret Geddes. When I was working on an authorised biography of Prince Philip's mother, one of the first things his archivist, the late Dame Anne Griffiths, told me was that one of the great sadnesses of Prince Philip's life was the death of his sister, made worse by the knowledge that she was pregnant. The baby was in fact born during the flight as a result of the trauma associated with the crash.

Prince Andrew did not see Prince Philip for the first time at the reception after the funeral. They travelled together to the funeral in Darmstadt.

The implication of this episode is that Prince Philip as good as killed his sister, which as the above facts show, is untrue.[1]

The point the episode wants to make is that Prince Philip was ill-treated by his father, and then did not hesitate to submit his son to the same unpleasant school life. When the fictional Prince Charles is upset and wimpy in the aeroplane, Prince Philip shouts at him that he is 'bloody wet'. When they arrive back at Windsor, Prince Philip runs off to play with Princess Anne, and Prince Charles is led forlornly into the castle.

Minor mistakes – Lord Mountbatten writes on crested paper, but the coat of arms is that of the Marlboroughs not the Mountbattens; Windsor Castle scenes were filmed at Belvoir Castle – usually with the Royal Standard hanging in the hall, but in one scene they failed to change it, and instead we see the Garter banner of one of the Dukes of Rutland.

EPISODE 10

'Mystery Man'

The first scene shows Prince Philip waking with a cricked neck, made worse by his subsequent exercises outdoors. He is sent off to see the osteopath, Dr Stephen Ward, who sorts him out, and then explains that the Prince is probably tense and that he could maybe help him. He invites him to one of his notorious parties, and there is mention of Christine Keeler and Mandy Rice-Davies. 'My neck's feeling better already,' says the Prince, seizing another opportunity for potential lascivious behaviour. It is not explicit that he does go, but he is soon heading off for weekends away and travel overseas, even when the Queen is pregnant with Prince Edward (informed of this good news by that homeopathic quack, Sir John Weir, who was not an obstetrician).

Moving on a year, John Profumo is in trouble, and is summoned for a chat over a game of billiards with Harold Macmillan, on his return from an afternoon on the grouse moors. Macmillan tells his wife that years in politics have taught him when a man is lying. She calls him 'a credulous, trusting fool'.

This is the swinging sixties. Lady Dorothy attends a performance of *Beyond the Fringe*, and persuades Macmillan to go along too. As ever, Peter Morgan is much more convincing when he is treating politics than the Royal Family. The Profumo/Stephen Ward drama is played out: the questioning of Christine Keeler, the arrest of Stephen Ward, and presently his trial and suicide. All this is fine.

Macmillan's resignation and the appointment of the Earl of Home as his successor is another theme. It is suggested that at first the Queen refused to accept Macmillan's resignation over the Profumo affair. What actually happened was that Macmillan wrote to the Queen in June 1963 apologising for the 'development of recent affairs', without offering to resign. He decided to step down in October following a prostate operation, realising that it was time to go. By citing ill-health he avoided being pushed out by dissidents in his party following the Profumo scandal.

There was a lot of political scheming behind the scenes, but Macmillan realised that the Palace wanted one name to be recommended as the next Prime Minister, not seven. So he prepared a memorandum which concluded that the Earl of Home should be sent for. He asked the Queen to visit him in hospital and gave her this advice (on 18 October) while he was still technically in office, and so she was constitutionally required to take it. While Macmillan may have been anxious to kill Rab Butler's chances of taking over, he was also keen not to put the Queen in a difficult position.

The Queen received Home later the same day and invited him to form an administration. The late Ben Pimlott described the Queen's acceptance of Home over Butler as 'the biggest political misjudgement of her reign', but Macmillan's biographer, D.R. Thorpe refuted this, not least since Butler's chances with the party were slim.

The possible involvement of Prince Philip and Stephen Ward is hinted at with no evidence to support it. In June 1963, at the height of the scandal, there were what Richard Davenport-Hines has called 'outrageous headlines for non-existent stories.' The *Daily Mirror* printed one: 'PRINCE PHILIP AND THE PROFUMO SCANDAL – RUMOUR UTTERLY UNFOUNDED.' The paragraphs that followed failed to specify any such imagined rumour.

Stephen Ward sketched numerous public figures, some better than others. He was given commissions by the *Illustrated London News* and the *Daily Telegraph*. His sitters included Princess Margaret, the Queen's uncle, the Duke of Gloucester, her aunt, the Princess Royal, and figures such as Archbishop Makarios, Nancy Astor and Sir John Rothenstein. He sketched Prince Philip. Amongst his more outré portraits is a naked Mandy Rice-Davies, reclining as if posing for a Lucian Freud portrait. Today Ward's pictures fetch thousands of pounds in the saleroom, but no one is suggesting that the late Duke of Gloucester or the late Princess Royal were frolicking in Lord Astor's swimming pool at Cliveden.

The episode heads towards its end, and the finale of the series, with the Queen confronting Prince Philip with the photograph of Ulanova from Episode 1. He sidesteps this, but asserts that he is ultimately the one person who is forever completely loyal to her. This would appear to be a sop from the film-makers, a curious back-tracking after spending a considerable part of twenty episodes painting him in dismal light.

Another minor mistake – Princess Marina complains of the noise as Princess Margaret's workmen modernise her apartment at Kensington Palace. She tells the Queen that this noise is even annoying the Gloucesters. 'Everything irritates the Gloucesters,' says the fictional Queen. It must have been very noisy, since the Gloucesters did not live at Kensington Palace then. They were some miles away in York House, St James's Palace.

ABOUT THE AUTHOR

In 2018 Hugo Vickers edited The Quest for Queen Mary (first published by Zuleika, and later by Zuleika/ Hodder), which was universally well reviewed and sold over 40,000 copies.

He is Chairman of the Commonwealth Walkway Trust and he was appointed an honorary Fellow of the Royal Canadian Geographical Society in 2019. He is a Deputy Lieutenant of the Royal County of Berkshire and has been Captain of the Lay Stewards of St. George's Chapel, Windsor, for 50 years.

He lives between London and Wiltshire, and has three grown-up children, Arthur, Alice and George.